Bollin
Valley

Bollin
Valley

From Macclesfield to the Ship Canal

Keith Warrender

Willow
PUBLISHING

Tops of Dunham Massey hall and stables from the Bridgewater Canal

Text copyright ©Keith Warrender 2013
Photographs ©Keith Warrender 2013 unless acknowledged
First published 2013 by Willow Publishing

Willow Publishing
36 Moss Lane, Timperley
Altrincham, Cheshire WA15 6SZ

ISBN 978-0-946361-45-8

Book designed by Keith Warrender
Printed by the Buxton Press

Dedicated to Ben, Sarah and Daniel
and families

Front cover: Weirs on the Bollin at Prestbury
Opposite title page: Styal cross
Title page: Footpath at Dunham Woodhouses

Contents

Introduction - 6

Bollin Valley map - 8

40 Years of Countryside Management - 10

Macclesfield Forest - 13

Tegg's Nose - 23

Langley and Sutton - 31

Macclesfield - 42

Prestbury - 53

Mottram St Andrew - 69

Wilmslow - 79

Styal - 101

Ringway - 115

Around Ashley - 121

Dunham Massey - 163

Little Bollington - 177

Warburton - 185

Acknowledgements - 206

Introduction

I was born within a few hundred yards of the River Bollin at stately Prestbury Hall. It sounds a grand introduction to the world in such an 'upmarket' location, however, this was an experience shared by many Manchester babies as you will read in the Prestbury section.

After spending my childhood in south Manchester, I came to live in Timperley near Altrincham where the Bollin was just a short car-ride away. As a keen walker and photographer, I found the valley a great place to explore. Then in 1984, I got to know the river even more closely after providing the photographs for Joan French's book 'Bollin Valley'. It took me to areas of the valley I had not been before and reminded me further what a fascinating and beautiful area it is. Joan's book quickly sold out and nothing has since been published specifically on the valley.

I have been giving illustrated talks on the Bollin to local groups for nearly ten years. Audiences enjoy seeing and hearing about the places they remember from childhood, and for others it is a reminder of places visited. But I have also been able to surprise people with stories and locations which they knew little of. I hope readers will also discover new things as they go through the book.

For many today, the valley is where they quickly access glorious countryside for exercise and relaxation. As I've talked to people while out walking, I realised that some are only familiar with the section where they live. This book may encourage you to enjoy the attractions of the rest of the valley.

The river used to have a number of mills along its route. Most of them have long since gone and so I have researched the history of these places, along with the stories of the people who lived in the great country estates close to the Bollin. Within the scope of this book, it has not been possible to go into great detail about places such as Styal and Dunham Massey, and readers are advised to look at the National Trust's and other publications listed at the end of the book.

I am delighted that the Bollin Valley Partnership has contributed an article, especially as this year marks their 40th anniversary. I am grateful for all their help in the preparation of this book and also acknowledge the generous assistance of many other individuals and organisations who have given of their time, photographs and documents for this publication which, I hope, will interest, inform and help you to enjoy this lovely valley.

Keith Warrender

Opposite page -
Top: Wilmslow Park
Left: Quarry Bank mill pool

This page -
Top: Riverside Park
Middle left: Tegg's Nose Country Park
Middle right: St Werburgh's Church, Warburton
Above: Sunbank Wood, Castle Mill

MANCHESTER SHIP CANAL

Rixton
Old Hall

Butchersfield
Canal

Bollin
Point

LYMM

Warburton

Heatley
Mill

Dunham
Woodhouses

Dunham
Town

BOWDON

HALE

Little
Bollington

Dunham
Massey

Watch
Hill

Ashley
Mill

Ashley
Hall

Ashley

HALE BARNS

Ross
Mill

Castle
Mill

Sunbank
Wood

Cotterill
Clough

Bollin Valley Partnership

The River Bollin

Bollin Valley Partnership

8

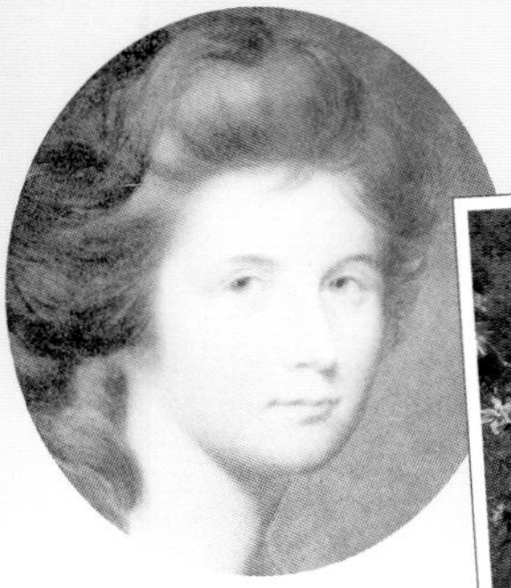

Quarry Bank Mill Archive, National Trust

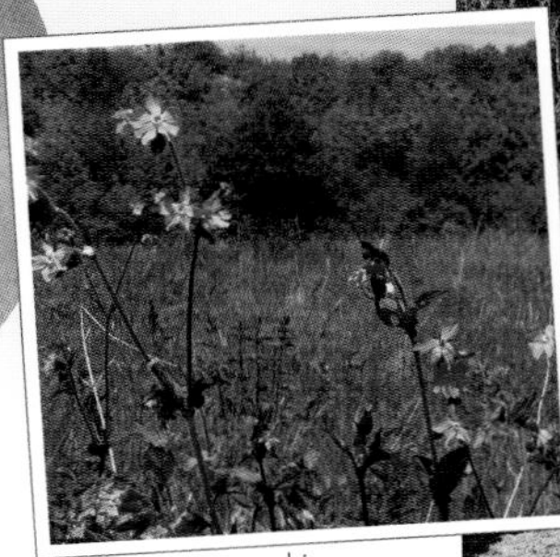

Bollin Valley Partnership

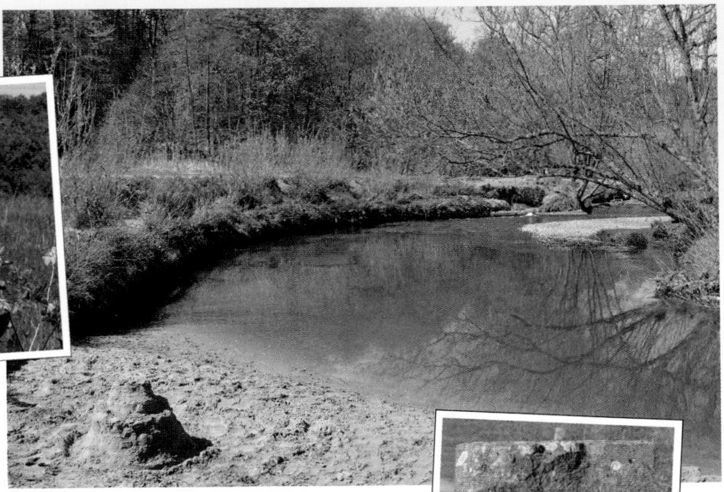

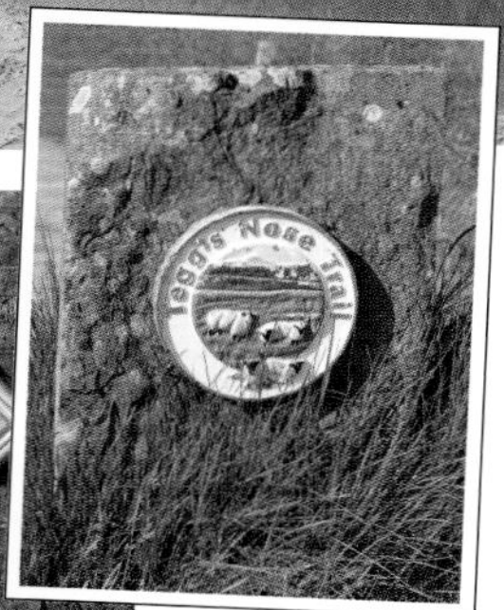
Teggs Nose Trail

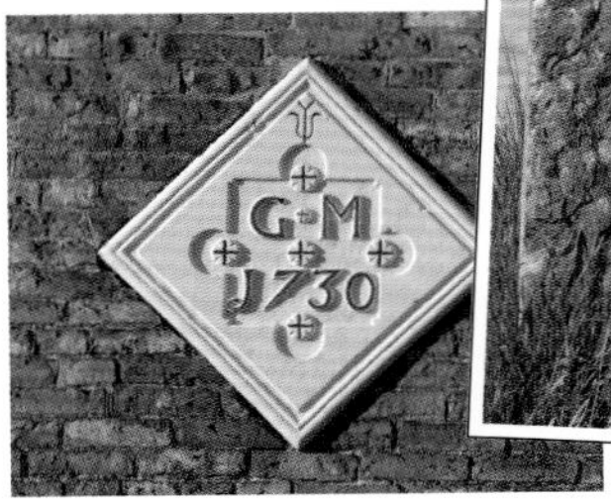
G M
1730

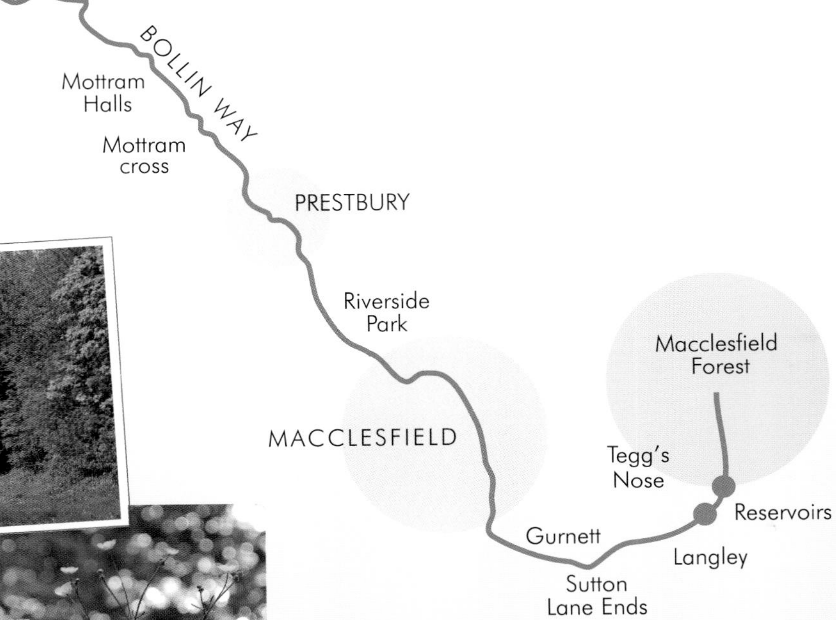
Manchester International Airport
Styal
Quarry Bank Mill
Dean Row
Wilmslow Park
The Carrs
Lindow
WILMSLOW
BOLLIN WAY
Mottram Halls
Mottram cross
PRESTBURY
Riverside Park
MACCLESFIELD
Macclesfield Forest
Tegg's Nose
Reservoirs
Gurnett
Langley
Sutton Lane Ends

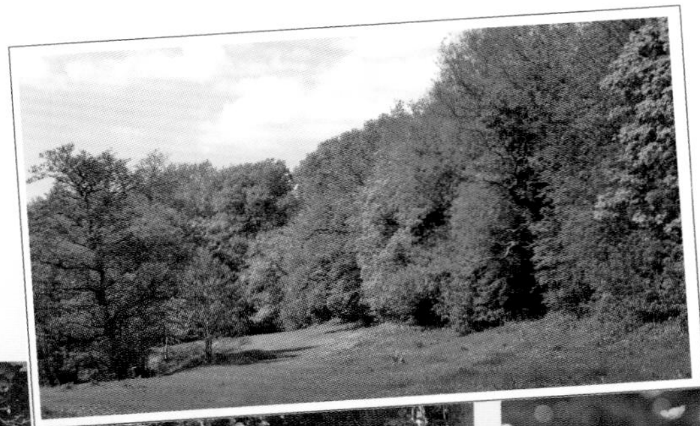

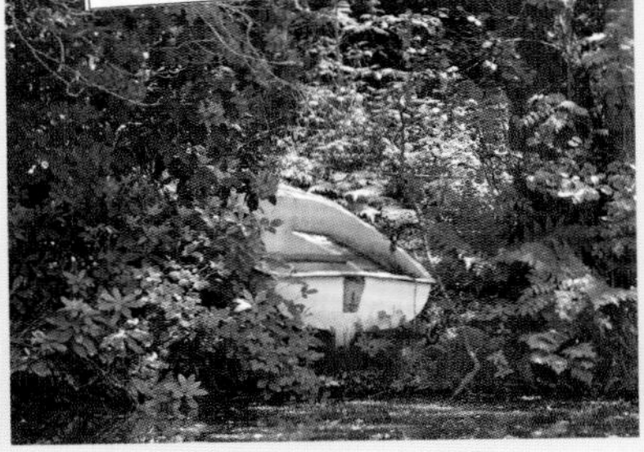

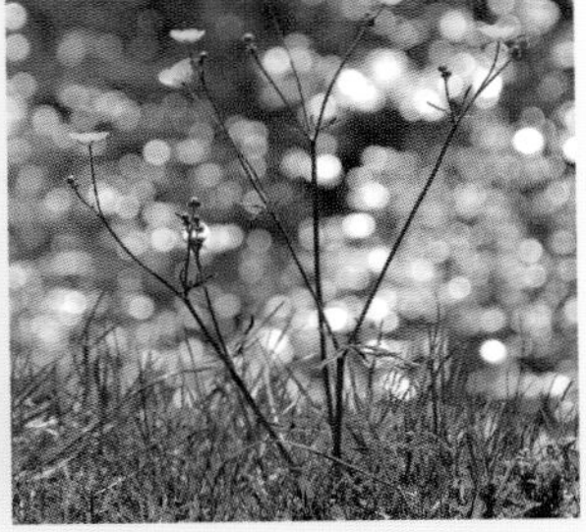

Bollin Valley Partnership - 40 Years of Countryside Management

Top Left: Footpath restoration, Pigginshaw Brook, Styal

Top right: Discovery Day Programme - family bike ride

Inset: Habitat restoration - control of invasive plants along the river

Below: River clean up with community group at the Carrs, Wilmslow

The Bollin Valley Project was formed in 1972 by agreement between Cheshire County Council and the Countryside Commission. It was an experiment into how the countryside could be managed to both accommodate the working environment and the increasing demand for countryside recreation. The first Project Officer was appointed in the autumn of that year. Forty years on, the Bollin Valley is still valued by residents, visitors and communities as a special place.

The Bollin Valley Project changed its name in the late 1990s to the Bollin Valley Partnership. Today the Partnership consists of a team of seven staff delivering a Countryside Management Service throughout the length of the Bollin Valley, from Macclesfield to the Manchester Ship Canal.

The work is varied, interesting and challenging, and a great deal has been achieved over the last forty years. Working with volunteers, schools, corporate organisations, partners and local people has helped to deliver many projects; the Discovery Day Programme of walks, countryside events and activities is a good example.

Acquiring external grants is vitally important to the success of delivering projects. Much of the long-distance footpath 'The Bollin Valley Way' was financed by external grants, and delivered by local people. The works involved upgrading and replacing many old wooden stiles with new kissing gates and surfacing wet areas of the path with gritstone for ease of walking. The Bollin

Valley Way is one of just a few 'new' long-distance footpaths in the area and is available for walkers' use. It provides beautiful views along the River Bollin, and gives the walkers a real sense of being out in the countryside.

In 1988 the then Bollin Valley Project bought its first Longhorn Cattle to help manage the new Macclesfield Riverside Park. The park is situated in Macclesfield and Prestbury along the banks of the river Bollin.

In 1988 Longhorn Cattle numbers were very low and using the cattle to graze the park helped contribute to the recovery of an English breed. Twenty-five years on, the cattle still play important role conserving the species-rich meadows at Macclesfield Riverside Park and also bring in valuable income which is used to fund the management of the Bollin Valley.

The water quality of the river Bollin has improved greatly over the years, bringing benefits to people and wildlife. In more recent years, otters have been recorded in the valley. This improvement should continue and offers more opportunities for other species as well as recreational opportunities for local communities.

Top: Bridge construction through a grant scheme

Middle: The Longhorn herd - conserving the meadows and providing income

Above: Discovery day programme - taster day for people with disabilities

Left: Invasive plant 'bashing' with corporate volunteers

Forestry and the landscape will always be important to the Partnership. In the early 1980s a great deal of work was carried out to control Dutch Elm disease; the loss of many magnificent old elms changed the landscape of the Bollin Valley. Today, the threat of ash dieback disease is another good example of why the work of the Partnership is so important in conserving the diversity of the landscape in the valley for future generations.

We are continuing to work with our communities, partners and volunteers, whilst adapting to change, taking funding opportunities and benefiting from an experienced, enthusiastic professional countryside management team. The future for the Bollin Valley, the landscape and the people who come and enjoy it, looks good!

TIM HARDING

Countryside Manager, Bollin Valley Partnership

Bollin Valley Partnership Partners: Cheshire East Council, Trafford Borough Council, The National Trust, Environment Agency

Top: Tree planting with community groups

Left: Litter picking with scouts

Below left: Bluebell survey with school children

Below right: River bank stabilisation work at the Carrs, Wilmslow

Right: Bollin Valley Way long distance footpath

MACCLESFIELD FOREST

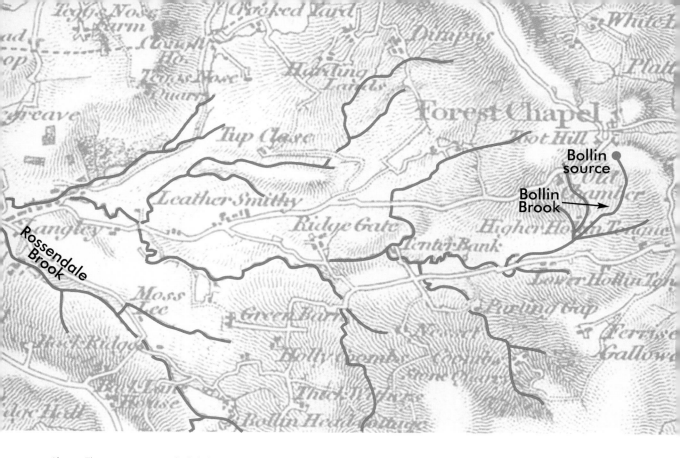

Above: The many streams which help form the river Bollin, highlighted on the 1800 OS map, before the building of the Trentabank and Ridgegate reservoirs. Note 'Bollinhead' at the bottom of the map which suggests another source of the river.

Below: Bollin Brook and two other streams empty into a pool

The river Bollin is 49km or just over thirty miles long. The official source of the Bollin is in a field close to the Forest Chapel. Here is the first sighting known as a 'wet flush' around 1280ft above sea level. On the Ordnance Survey map it is shown lower down the hill as 'Bollin Brook' and then converges with two other streams (not shown on the Ordnance Survey Explorer map) which empty through a pipe into a pool by the side of a track. The other two watercourses would seem contenders to be called 'the source'. One springs up at the edge of the woodland by the Standing Stone car park, while the other originates on the southern slopes of Toot Hill.

The augmented Bollin Brook moves further through Macclesfield Forest before joining Trentabank Reservoir, which is fed by another stream from Toot Hill. Brooks from the direction of Buxtors Hill and south of the road from Trentabank to Standing Stones also flow into the reservoir.

Before the construction of Trentabank Reservoir, Bollin Brook flowed past the settlements of Lower Hollintongue, Twelve Ashes and Trentabank and into Ridgegate Reservoir, known in 1875 as the Langley Reservoir.

Above top: Source of the Bollin, just below the barn at Toothill farm
Above left: Bollin Brook descends to meet other streams
Above right: A stream which rises just below Standing Stones to link with Bollin Brook
Left: Origins of the stream which rises at Toot Hill

Macclesfield Forest Chapel

The Chapel is best known for the annual rushbearing service in August when, as a celebration of spiritual renewal, the old rushes are replaced. It is not known when the tradition began here, but it originates from the days when the bare floor of the chapel was covered in rushes to make it warmer and to sweeten the air. The rushes are cut from nearby marshes, plaited and made into decorations interwoven with flowers. Following the complete rebuilding of the chapel in 1834, there was no further need for the rushes, but the custom was either maintained or begun at this point.

Top: 2013 Rushbearing service

Inset: Rev Gage Earl Freeman - vicar here for over thirty years

The service is a highlight in the life of the valley and it packs the chapel. They sing the Rushbearing hymn: *'Our fathers these same floors have trod, Whereon these rushes have been laid, And now within the Realms of God, From earth's sorrows free are made.'* The first part of the service is relayed by speakers to people outside the chapel, and then the message is given by the preacher in the churchyard, standing on a table tomb. Each year, a group of walkers make their way to the service from Tegg's Nose. The rushes and decorations can be seen by visitors for several days after the service.

The normally peaceful ceremony was disrupted in 1848 in a 'memorable rushbearing' - possibly due to drunken behaviour. No details of the incident have survived but the chapel records show that broken windows had to be repaired and a new lock put on the door.

During the 1888 service, the local police constable spotted a notorious local poacher passing by. The constable went to arrest the man but he resisted and members of the crowd helped to subdue him while the service continued. Afterwards, the vicar persuaded the man to go quietly into police custody.

Locals believed that the date of the ceremony was linked to the nearest Sunday after the twelfth so that the patron, the Earl of Derby, could attend while he stayed at nearby Crag Hall for the grouse shooting season.

Although the datestone on the chapel states it was built in 1673, the first minister was not appointed until 1685. The 'SS' on the datestone

Decorations for the Rushbearing sevice

may refer to the church's name of St Stephen. The Rev Gage Earl Freeman, who was the vicar for over thirty years from 1856, was an authority on falconry and wrote the books 'Falconry: Its Claims, History and Practice' and 'Practical Falconry'. He would be frequently seen on the moors with falcons on his arms ready to supply him with game. For many years he was the main contributor on falconry matters for the 'Field' magazine. He also wrote 'Mount Carmel', a story of modern English life, as well as a number of books of poetry which won him the Seatonian Prize on four occasions for the best English poem on a sacred subject. The Rev Freeman died at Penrith age 83 in 1903 and was buried at Forest Chapel.

The chapel is built from stone known as Chatsworth Grit, and stands at 1282 ft above sea level. Although an impressive setting in summer, it can be a bleak isolated hamlet in bad weather. The burial registers have records of people perishing in the snow and not being found for weeks afterwards. The graveyard is noted for the wide variety of wild flowers growing there until they are cut down in August.

Macclesfield Forest

It was once part of a Royal Forest which stretched south to the Stafford moorlands. The area belonged to the Earl of Chester until 1237 when it passed to the Crown after he died without children. King John, Edward I, Richard II and Henry V are all thought to have hunted here.

Earthworks at Toot Hill

Although it was called a 'forest' it was mainly moorland with the natural wooded areas on the higher ground of Macclesfield Forest. Here, around 200 head of deer were allowed to roam in readiness for hunting by the King. There was a large fenced-off section known as 'The Chase of the Coombs' set apart for the Royal hunt. This was thought to be a broad area of the Bollin Valley from east of the present town of Macclesfield, stretching up to Buxtors Hill and Toot Hill to the east of Macclesfield Forest.

The forest was for royal pleasure and recreation, and there were severe penalties for anyone caught poaching. A man found in possession of a stag in 1278 was imprisoned and all his goods impounded. The Davenport family of Capesthorne Hall, as Sergeants of the Forest, would dispense justice. This is reflected in the family

The mysterious name of 'Bollin'

The origins and meaning of 'Bollin' are uncertain. Over the centuries it has been spelt in many different ways, including: Bolyne 1190, Bolyn 1220, and Bollen 1577. The most popular interpretation is that it means 'torrent of eels'. 'Bol' means eel in old English, and 'hlynn' refers to a torrent or noisy stream. The Bollin changes from a placid stream into a turbulent watercourse in times of heavy rain, and eels were once trapped here under the mud.

It is obvious how Little Bollington near Dunham Massey got its name with the river Bollin flowing through the village. Not so clear is why Bollington near

Macclesfield is so named, as it stands on the River Dean which joins the Bollin at Wilmslow. It would seem that in the past, both the streams had the same name but for different reasons. 'Bol' may have referred to someone who settled here, 'ing' means belonging to, and 'ton' means community - Bollington.

At Macclesfield, the river was known either as 'The Bollin' or 'The Jordan' in the 1828 Pigot directory. Macclesfield historian Isaac Finney suggested that the Bollin had been only known by its present name at the point where it was joined by the River Dean further along at Wilmslow.

crest which shows a thief with a rope around his neck. The Downes family of Taxal had the privilege of 'rousing the game' at the Royal Hunt and holding the stirrup when the King mounted his horse.

There is much discussion about the location of a lodge in the Forest for the King and his entourage, including stabling. The old hunting lodge known as 'The Chamber in the Forest', is shown on maps up to 1750 but its exact location is not known today. It may have been at Toot Hill - 'Toot' means 'lookout'. The Toot Hill earthworks are generally thought to be the remains of a deerpound or 'buckstall'. However it has been pointed out that it was more likely to be sited at nearby 'Bucksta's Hill'. During the hunt, the deer would be chased into the pound - a fenced enclosure - to be trapped alive. The earthworks therefore may have been a temporary fortification, with possibly the King's Lodge nearby, although archaeological digs have not confirmed this. It is known that a similar 'King's Chamber' at Delamere Forest was at the highest point close to a Saxon fortification.

Top: Trentabank Reservoir, completed in 1929, was officially opened by the Duke of Gloucester. It holds 130,000 gallons of water and is 59ft deep in parts. In the centre right of the photo are the remains of the route of the old road before the reservoir was built, and the builder's light railway.

Above: Forest trail near Standing Stones

Top: Trentabank, Ridgegate and Bottoms reservoirs and Tegg's Nose. Around 528,000 gallons of compensation water from Tegg's Nose and Bottoms reservoirs is discharged daily into the river Bollin

Above: The Bollin in Macclesfield Forest

Above right: Trentabank reservoir

Right: Short length of two ft gauge track from the Trentabank Reservoir light railway near the Forest Office

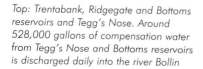

20

Records state that in 1648 a group of royalists broke through a guard at Whaley Bridge to reach the lodge at Macclesfield Forest and made off with all the horses to Pontefract. Later the forest area was enclosed into private ownership. In 1590 Queen Elizabeth permitted Henry Earl of Derby to 'disafforest' the former hunting area, and many farmhouses were built.

Macclesfield Forest is also the name of the chapelry served by St Stephen's Church, known by many as Forest Chapel. United Utilities own the forest, and parts of it are designated sites of biological importance. Conifers planted between 1930 and 1950 protect water catchment areas from pollution. The nature reserve is managed by the Cheshire Wildlife Trust at Trentabank with a heronry, the largest in the Peak District, and a herd of over fifty red deer.

Inset: Head forester, Tom Burke in 1951. He succeeded his father who had worked there since 1925

Middle right: The remains of Ferriser farm. This and a closed bungalow near Trentabank Visitor Centre are the only two remaining properties in the forest

Below: Wood anemone

Bollin Valley Partnership

United Utilities

Forest tornado

'20th June 1662 ... in the forest of Maxfield, there arose a great pillar of smoke, in height like a steeple, and twenty yards broad, which making most hideous noise, went along the ground six or seven miles, levelling all in the way; it threw down fences and stone walls and carried stones great distances, but happening upon the moorish ground not inhabited, it did less hurt. The terrible noise so frighted the cattle that they ran away and were preserved; it passed over a corn field and laid it even with the ground as if trodden down by feet; it went through a wood and turned up a hundred trees by the roots and left a tree in the middle of a field which it had brought from some other place.'

(From an account given by the Minister of Taxal Church)

Top: Ridgegate reservoir, constructed between 1850 - 52, provides drinking water for Macclesfield. It holds over 120,000 gallons of water and is 38ft at its deepest point. In 1878 during repairs, a Celtic urn was uncovered, containing the burnt bones of a young man and a flint arrowhead.

Above: Ridgegate reservoir, from Tegg's Nose. Beside the reservoir is 'Leather's Smithy' pub which is named after William Leather, a farmer, who obtained a licence in 1821 to sell ale and porter. When it was put up for sale in 1883, the reservoirs were said to attract anglers from all over Britain.

TEGG'S NOSE

Above and below: Examples of the machinery used in quarries including a crane for lifting the larger blocks of stone, and the red stone crusher which produced enough to fill five lorries daily

Below: The huge space where the best stone was quarried

Tegg's Nose

The unusual name may have derived from Tegge an early Norse settler, although 'Tegge' also means young sheep, and could refer to the sheep-like shape of the headland. 'Naze' means headland or outcrop. Stone, known as Chatsworth Grit, has been quarried here since the 15th century. It has a distinctive pink colour and was noted for its durability, and used by Macclesfield Corporation for paving, including the '108 Steps', and the facing of the Library and College of Further Education. Some of Cambridge's colleges were restored with it and the stone was also used at the Marine Gardens, Douglas, Isle of Man. The best quality stone came from the southern part of the quarry where there is a cavernous hole. Later in the 1920s and 1930s there was a growing demand for smaller crushed stone used in road and airfield building, and also the breakwater at Douglas. This was quarried along a 100 yard section below the Tegg's Nose summit.

Quarrying work was dangerous and difficult but it didn't stop the quarrymen exerting themselves further, with contests to lift the heaviest barrowload of stone, or have a lunchtime tug of war. In the pub they enjoyed arm wrestling and 'poker wrestling'. They supplemented their low wages by polishing monumental stones, snaring rabbits and killing foxes.

The quarryman's day started at 7am in the summer, which may have included a walk of several miles to get there. They worked until 6pm with a 10-minute break for breakfast and one hour for lunch. On Saturdays, they finished at noon, and they had a week's break during the Macclesfield silk workers' traditional 'Barnaby holidays' in June and July. Many of the men contracted the lung disease silicosis through breathing in the stone dust, and were laid off. Annual medical checks were introduced, and quarrymen given the all-clear would celebrate at the Setter Dog pub. They often worked in atrocious weather conditions on the exposed site and could be blown over by the wind.

Tegg's Nose quarry was at its peak during the 1800s with around twenty men working there, but in the twentieth century production became more expensive and the site was shut down in 1920. Five years later, it was re-opened by Ashton and Holmes who took up a 14-year lease. Mechanisation began around 1938 with a large crusher to break up the stone for road-making. However, when the company had to supply a special size of stone for Prestbury sewage works, it was more economical to use 'handknappers' to manually break up the stone. During the last War, to increase production, American servicemen worked alongside the local quarryworkers, bringing with them 20 lorries, an excavator and a compressor.

Stone which was of no use was dumped down the hillside

Blasting, introduced on Sunday mornings, caused not only noise problems in the locality but the hazard of rocks rolling into the valley damaging buildings, and also hitting power lines causing electricity cuts. 'Big Lol', one of the characters at the quarry, used a hefty sledge-hammer that was too heavy for everyone else. Another quarryman used his blasting expertise to blow 62 safes, before he was arrested.

After the War, the company found it difficult to recruit workers prepared to endure the unpleasant conditions at Tegg's Nose. Also, there were planning restrictions in the 1950s which prevented further quarrying on the west side of the hill. As a result quarrying ended here about 1955 and Cheshire County Council opened it as a country park in 1972, and the site is now managed by the Cheshire East Countryside Ranger Service. The 35-mile Gritstone Trail between Disley and Kidsgrove passes over Tegg's Nose.

Above top: Panorama from Tegg's Nose - Shuttlingsloe (left), Ridgegate Reservoir and Sutton Common BT tower (right) built around 1960

Middle: Mountain pansies at Tegg's Nose

Left: 'Wavy wall' built by stonewaller John Robertson next to the visitor centre

Bollin Valley Partnership

Above: harebells and cowberry

Left: Jodrell Bank from Tegg's Nose

Overleaf: Tegg's Nose reservoir and
Bottoms reservoir from Tegg's Nose

Above: Tegg's Nose Reservoir built 1871

Right and below right: 'Toposcope' viewpoint, derived from the Greek 'topos' meaning place - designed by artist and designer Reece Ingram. Ten spy-holes in the drystone circle line up with landmarks, including his home in Macclesfield.

Below: Milestone just outside the entrance to the car park

Below middle: Visitors are encouraged to read or borrow a book which can be returned or replaced

To London 168 miles

LIBRARY

in the LANDSCAPE

My House

LANGLEY & SUTTON

Tegg's Nose Reservoir

The Bollin as it passes under Hole House Lane

Previous page: Macclesfield canal near Sutton Hall. Above: Overflow from Tegg's Nose and Bottoms reservoirs

Langley Hall

The hall dates back to before 1651, when it passed into the ownership of the Clowes family through the marriage of William to Katherine Yeveley of Langley. The 1696 shell-hood over the door indicates when the hall was rebuilt. During roof alterations in the 1800s there was evidence that cock-fighting had taken place there. The hall and estate, which included a water-powered loom works, bleaching and print works, farm houses, St Dunstan public house and cottages, was sold by the Clowes family around 1808 to David Yates, a Manchester silk throwster. The first mills in Langley were built between 1800 and 1805 at Bollinhead.

The Langley Print Works was founded about 1820 by silk textile printer William Smith in outbuildings close to the hall. Then in 1826 he and John Smith built the mill at Cock Hall Lane. Smith's grandson

Left: Rossendale Brook flows through the grounds to join the Bollin

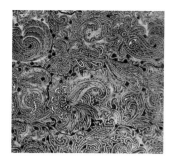

Above: Examples of Whiston's hand blocks at Macclesfield Silk Museum

William Whiston took over the business in 1870 and it expanded into the world's biggest silk printing, dyeing and finishing company.

They were especially known for the ornate designs in copper and brass for hand block printing. It is claimed that these beautiful works of craftsmanship could be found on the walls of many former workers' homes in Langley. Large quantities of the blocks were melted down to make weapons during World War I, and others were destroyed because of the lack of storage space. Surviving blocks are now much sought after by collectors. Macclesfield Silk Heritage Museum has an extensive collection. However, the dyes from the works caused much pollution turning the Bollin different colours.

The works, later known as Brocklehurst, Whiston Amalgamated closed in 1964. The site was then occupied by the Macclesfield company Ernest Scragg and Sons Ltd who made textile machinery. As the business grew, they built an extension in 1970, with a single-span roof which was the biggest of its kind in Europe. Business success continued after its amalgamation with the Swiss company Rieter AG, until its closure in 2005. The buildings were demolished and it is now partly the site of the Mill Fold residential development.

William Smith lived at Langley Hall at the time of the 1851 census, and also in 1861 when he employed 22 men and 2 boys at the works. The Cooper and Wilson farming families lived at the hall up to the late 1880s and then it was split into several tenements to become the home of textile workers. Harry Millward, a block cutter at Whiston's mill who lived there, was a chorister at St Paul's Church in Macclesfield. It was estimated he had walked over 25,000 miles to attend 5000 services by the time of his retirement from the choir in 1927. He was greatly respected in the district and was presented with gifts of money and an armchair for his dedication to the church. A friend said that Harry made the long journey on foot to the services whatever the weather. Harry died age 47, six years later. Today, the hall is still split into apartments.

Weavers' cottages, Langley

**Langley Hall -
owners and occupiers**

1828 - Henry Yates

1851 - William Smith

1871 - Thomas Cooper, farmer

1881 - Thomas Cooper,
& Ralph Steel

1883 - William Wilson, farmer

1891 - John J Davidson,
silk colour mixer

1901 - Harry Millward,

1902 - Henry Millward

1924 - Henry Millward
and Charles Frederick Plant

1934 - William Hammond

Above left and right: From Langley towards Tegg's Nose

Langley Mill, built in 1872 opposite the village hall, was a supplier to the textile printing trade. *Albert Mill*, erected c1805, had a water-powered water wheel which was sold as scrap in 1939 to assist the war effort. The building was demolished in 1952. *Bollinhead Mill*, built between 1800 and 1805, and powered by water wheel, produced tape, and is now site of the house 'Pres du Doit'. Furniture making also took place there from 1887 by John Thomas Moore who made adjustable chairs and tables and an early version of the deck-chair. His 'Hygienic' rocking chair was advertised as suitable for people with 'sluggish or constipated bowels'. The mill was reduced to a single storey in 1914. *Riverside Mills*, behind Langley Hall built c1837 as a silk finishing works is now an educational centre. *River Mills* constructed in 1906 as the Hollins Steam Laundry, was taken over by Whistons in 1918 and used today for screen printing.

River Bollin, Langley

Tunnicliffe watercolour - 'Ploughing
Bullock's meadow at Sutton'

Charles Tunnicliffe

Charles Tunnicliffe was described by the naturalist Peter Scott as 'the greatest wild-life artist of the twentieth century'. He was born at Langley in 1901, the son of a shoemaker. Soon afterwards the family moved in as tenants of the 20-acre Lane Ends Farm where he grew up with his four sisters. Even at an early age there was a desire to sketch the world around him. He made chalk drawings of the farm animals on a wooden shed next to the house, and which overlooked the road, much to his father's displeasure. Every scrap piece of paper was used for pencil drawings as well as the white-washed walls of the shippons and stables.

Charles Tunnicliffe

To his great delight, his parents bought him paints and sketchbooks the next Christmas. These he filled with pictures of the livestock, including the neighbour's bull which broke into their fields. At the village school, the highlight of the week was the day they had memory drawing and he would create wild beasts, Cowboys and Indians and of course farm animals. At home he contributed to the running of the farm, milking the cows and delivering cans of milk before he went to school.

Tunnicliffe's headmaster recognised his great artistic talent and urged his parents to send him to Macclesfield School of Art, although a local farmer had not been very encouraging when he said to Charles, 'Any fool can wag a pencil Charley - but it takes a good man to muck out a cow shed!'. Fortunately, Margaret his mother was determined that her son should fulfil his potential and he was awarded a place and a scholarship at Macclesfield School of Art in 1915.

Tunnicliffe was an exceptional student and went on to pass the exam to London's Royal College of Art. City life did not appeal to him but he worked hard developing his artistic and craft skills. Extra money supplementing the £80 a year grant was made by producing etchings. After college he made a living with part-time teaching at Woolwich and also continued to producing etchings.

In 1928 he returned to Macclesfield and married Winifred Wonnacot, a ceramist and fellow student from the RCA. Working in his back garden shed, he became a noted commercial illustrator for the producers of cattle food, and seed and fertiliser merchants. Tunnicliffe had his first one-man show in London in 1938. He was also in demand as a book illustrator, his first being the classic 'Tarka the Otter' by Henry Williamson. Charles also wrote his own books. 'My Country Book', written in 1942, is a fascinating account of his early memories, with many of his fine illustrations.

During WW2 he taught at Manchester Grammar School and continued to draw the wildlife of Cheshire, but after holidaying in Anglesey he felt the need for a change of scene. In 1947 he and

Below: The wooden shed on which Tunicliffe made some of his early drawings

Below left: Tunicliffe illustration of Lane Ends farm

Below right: Tunnicliffe's former home is now Lane Ends farm shop

The Estate of CF Tunnicliffe

The Estate of CF Tunnicliffe

Tunnicliffe's OBE on display at
West Park Museum, Macclesfield

1954 Royal Academy show

Winifred went to live at Shorelands in Malltraeth in Anglesey with beautiful peaceful surroundings and lots of wildlife nearby.

When he was awarded an OBE in 1978, he was typically unassuming about it, commenting that he found it strange to be honoured for something he loved doing. Tunnicliffe was a frequent exhibitor at the Royal Academy and became a Royal Academican in 1954. The RSPB awarded him their gold medal in 1975. He spent forty years making a collection of measured drawings from dead birds sent to him. Many of these unique drawings were featured in a special RA exhibition in 1974. Anglesey Council acquired the work in 1981 and a part of it is now on permanent display at Oriel Ynes Môn near Llangefni.

Towards the end of his life he had sight problems and spent time organising his work. Charles Tunnicliffe died in 1979, shortly after being filmed for a television programme. Those who knew him described him as kind and generous. John Huddleston, his great nephew, remembered looking forward to visiting him in Anglesey. Charles was quite a private sort of person but would always find time to chat about art. He had a big library of books on art, enjoyed explaining the techniques used by Picasso, and passionately believed that art should be available for everyone to see.

Etching of his friend and neighbour's farm - John Bullock

Charles Tunnicliffe was not a recluse, but he had to work hard for long hours to earn a living and was content with a circle of friends that included ex-teaching colleagues and fellow artists.

Contemporaries in the art-world have commented on how Tunnicliffe so successfully captured the movement of wild creatures, and on his flawless draughtsmanship. Also few others have been able to portray the ripples, sparkle and shimmer of water in the way that he did. His work, which occasionally comes up for auction, continues to be sought after.

Right: The river Bollin as it passes under the Macclesfield canal at Gurnett. 77 vessels in procession passed over the aqueduct on the day of the canal's opening in 1831.

Below: Inscription over a garage that James Brindley, the pioneering engineer of canals, worked here for seven years. Brindley is said to have rescued Bennett's business by memorising details of another mill's machinery and then applied his knowledge to install a new waterwheel. After Bennett's death, Brindley completed the outstanding contracts before setting up his own business in Leek.

Bottom and inset: Jarman farm - once the home of John Bullock, friend of Charles Tunnicliffe. 'Jarman' comes from the 16th century Germyn family who lived here. Within the farm is the remains of a medieval moat. Jarman has been a dairy farm for many years but today it is a popular site for caravanners, campers and anglers.

ON THESE PREMISES
1733 ~ 1740
JAMES BRINDLEY,
THE FAMOUS CIVIL ENGINEER
AND CANAL BUILDER, SERVED
AS APPRENTICE TO ABRAHAM
BENNETT.

Sutton Hall

The estate can be traced back to the 12th century Sutton family, although the present building could be from the 16th century. The line of Suttons continued until 1601 when it passed into the ownership of the Davenports of Bramhall. The family were Roman Catholic sympathisers and during the period of Catholic suppression the chapel next to the hall was used for secret celebrations of the mass by the local community. Later alterations to the hall revealed a priest hole, a hiding place if the authorities came looking for the resident priest. The chapel was used until 1720 for this purpose when the owner, Lord Fauconberg, left the Catholic Church after being heavily fined and his lands confiscated for his religious beliefs. Over the following forty years it was used by the Established Church. After it ceased to be used for worship, the benches and the marble altar top were taken to Chelford Chapel.

Sutton family coat of arms

Ralph Holinshed, thought to have been born at the hall in the 16th century, was a scholar whose chronicles were used as the historical source for many of Shakespeare's plays. Holinshed worked for Reginald Wolfe, a London printer who was preparing a history of the world from The Flood to Queen ELizabeth, but Wolfe died in 1573 before it was finished. Holinshed and others were given permission to finish the British section and it was published as 'The Chronicles of England, Scotland and Ireland' in 1577.

The Lords Lucan were next to take ownership of the hall by marriage. Lady Lucan, the wife of the Earl, was said to be rather eccentric and used to be taken by sedan chair between home and the church at Macclesfield. This inspired a local childrens' rhyme: *'Lady Lucan sits in a sedan, As fair as a lily, as white as a swan, A pair of green gloves to doff and to don.'* In 1815 she let the hall and twelve acres of land.

The Lucans gained notoriety because George Bingham, the 3rd Earl, ordered the disastrous charge of the Light Brigade during the Crimean War in 1854 in which the cavalry suffered heavy casualties. In 1974, family descendant Lord Lucan, the 7th Earl, made international news after his sudden disappearance following the murder of his children's nanny. In spite of reported sightings around the world his whereabouts have never been officially confirmed.

George Bingham

Sutton Hall was occupied by the Bent family for over seventy years. This included three unmarried sisters, Frances, Sarah and Maria, from around 1831 onwards up to the death of Maria in 1901 aged 96. She was well-known and respected locally and generous to the needy. James Theodore Bent, the sisters' nephew who held the lease to the hall, was a frequent visitor. With his wife Mabel, he travelled the world searching out the remains of lost civilizations, writing about his experiences and archaeological finds. Although he had no formal training in the subject, his work was favourably received by the experts. His 1892 book 'The Ruined Cities of Mashonaland', about the newly found ruins of a city known as Great Zimbabwe, was initially a success but later archaeologists criticised his methods, accusing him of damaging both the sites and the recovered artefacts.

James and Mabel continued on their travels, exploring South Arabia and publishing their findings. However during a further tour of this area in 1897 they contracted malaria and quickly returned home to London, but James died within a few days. Mabel, who had contributed much to her late husband's books through her journals and photography, then went on to have her own 'Travel Chronicles' published. They are regarded as classic travel accounts and are still available today. Mabel lived to the age of 83, but became resentful that her husband's achievements had not been more fully recognised. She paid for a stained glass memorial window to her husband at St James Church, Sutton.

James Bent memorial,
St James Church, Sutton

Above left: Sutton Hall
Above right: Former chapel entrance

John Ridgway - his great grandfather, Job, founded the pottery works at Stoke in 1802

Sutton Hall

The hall was sold by the Lucans to local industrialist William Whiston JP in 1895 who had the hall restored. By 1906 it had become the residence of John Ridgway JP, co-owner of the family firm of Ridgway Pottery in Hanley, Stoke. His grandfather, John, had been appointed as official potter to Queen Victoria in 1851.

Leonard Lockheed Armitage and family came to live at the hall around 1912. He ran a cotton manufacturing business with mills at Farnworth and Manchester. He was popular with farmers because of his interest in agricultural matters, being patron of the local farmers' association and a member of the Sutton Bull Society. He loved horses, was a member of the hunt, chairman of the parish council and manager of the area's C of E schools. When he died in 1917 this prominent, genial character was much missed by the local community.

By 1950, the hall was unoccupied and bought by Charles Lomas, a Knight Commander of the Order of St Gregory - a high papal office - in order to restore the old Catholic Chapel. It had been used for many years as a barn and timber store. An altar was restored at the east end of the chapel, and several unglazed window openings uncovered. Evidence was also found of a room or balcony over the entrance at the west end. An old miniature lych-gate next to the chapel led to a former burial ground. After Lomas's death in 1961 the property was given to the Catholic order of the Sisters of Charity who were there until 1976. They received a £48 grant in 1973 towards the cost of £243 to repair the roof and walls. The hall later became a hotel and in 2009 it was opened by Brunning & Price as a pub, after renovations costing around £3million.

MACCLESFIELD

Macclesfield

The market town was granted its borough charter in the 13th century and is sometimes nicknamed 'Silk Town' because it became the biggest producer of silk in the world. Charles Roe opened the first silk mill at Park Green in 1756 and silk throwing mills were built alongside the river Bollin and Dams Brook. The sudden rise in demand for silk led manufacturers to send out an appeal to parents and guardians for up to 5000 young people between the ages of seven and twenty to come and work in Macclesfield. In the 1850s there were over 200 companies involved in the silk trade around the Macclesfield area.

The story of Macclesfield silk is explained at Paradise Mill on Park Lane which is now an industrial museum with the top floor preserved

as a handloom weaving room, and also at Park Lane Galleries and the Heritage Centre on Roe Street. West Park Museum has a fine collection of the work of wild life artist Charles Tunnicliffe amongst its exhibits.

Previous page: Riverside Park

Above: Waters Green - once the site of summer and Christmas fairs

Right: Paradise Mill

Below: Park Green used to be an open meadow, and traditionally a venue for public meetings. The war memorial was unveiled in 1921 before a crowd of 20,000 people.

The Bollin Trail through Macclesfield

An exploration of Macclesfield's heritage along the banks of the river Bollin

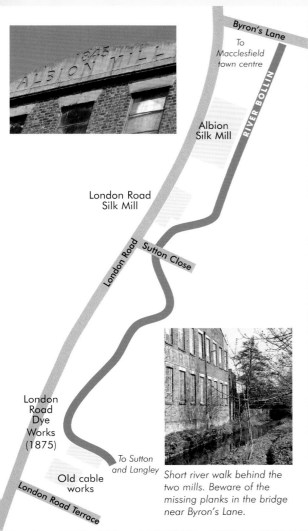

Albion silk mill and London Road mill dominate the southern approach to the town along London Road

London Road silk mill had specially strengthened flooring and cast iron columns to support the power weaving machinery introduced in 1901. Note the carved timber brackets supporting the roof.

Short river walk behind the two mills. Beware of the missing planks in the bridge near Byron's Lane.

45

Silk mill, Pool Street

Weavers' cottages, Pool Street

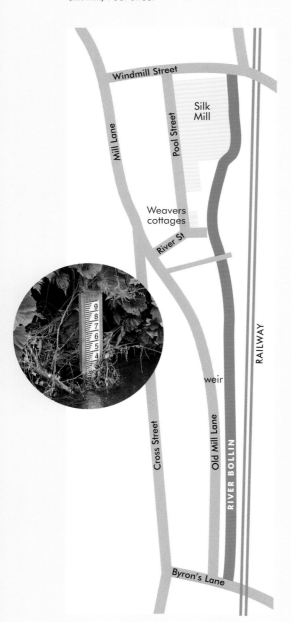

The river Bollin by Old Mill Lane

Left: Park Green House with the unusual curved gables, built 1720, was the home of John Firth, a surgeon. In May 1871, he and his wife died following a carriage accident. Their horse suddenly went out of control as they drove down Mill Street, crashing into iron posts at Park Green.

It was next occupied by Firth's practice partner Henry Fernie, physician and surgeon at Macclesfield Infirmary. He was a great admirer of Charles Dickens and collected everything written by the great author.

Dr Charles Averill who later lived there was a surgeon at the Infirmary, a JP and Colonel in the Army Medical Staff. He also wrote a book on field sanitation for territorial officers.

36 Park Green became the town's first lending library in 1770 and later a gentleman's club. The silk union workers' office formed in 1826 was at number 38.

One of two surviving doorways from the former Methodist church next to Frost's mill

Macclesfield Silk Museum

Georgian frontage of Park Green mill built 1785, now demolished, powered from the Bollin. Frost's Yarns closed in 1971 after 100 years of production.

Brook Street
Sunderland Street
Park Green House
36 and 38
Park Green
War memorial
Chapel mill
Park Green
Site of former Park Green silk mill
Bank Street
Mill Lane
THE SILK ROAD
RIVER BOLLIN
Waterside
Victoria silk mill
Windmill Street

Waterside was once known for the poor state of housing and overcrowding

Victoria mills built c1823, thought to have been one of the first in Macclesfield to have the French Jacquard looms. On the left is the engine house extending from the main mill.

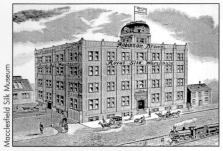

The former Royal Silk Warehouse, owned by Robinson Brown - the only one of its kind in East Cheshire, built in 1903. Its mail order catalogue made it nationally known. Note the initials of the owner's daughters on the pillars at the entrance. Later the building was occupied by the Castle Shoe Company, and is now a hotel.

Waters Green - former common land where the Bollin used to frequently flood. A number of brooks flow underground into the river at this point.

Gas Rd

Royal Silk Warehouse

Arighi Bianchi

BUXTON RD

Waters Green

Station

THE SILK ROAD

Cuckstoolpit Hill

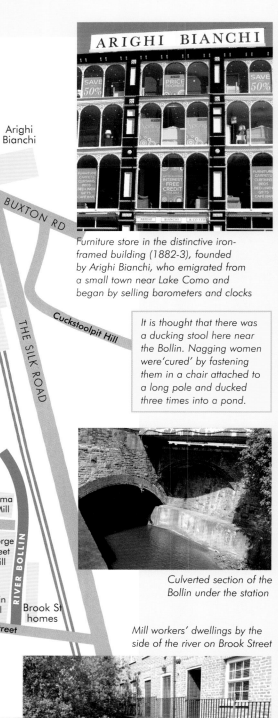

ARIGHI BIANCHI

Furniture store in the distinctive iron-framed building (1882-3), founded by Arighi Bianchi, who emigrated from a small town near Lake Como and began by selling barometers and clocks

It is thought that there was a ducking stool here near the Bollin. Nagging women were 'cured' by fastening them in a chair attached to a long pole and ducked three times into a pond.

John Wesley frequently preached at the chapel. During a service in 1798 people panicked when they wrongly thought a balcony was going to collapse. People died as they were trampled on, or jumped out of windows.

Wesleyan Chapel

Sunderland Street

Pickford Street

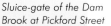

Dam brook

Alma Mill

George Street

George Street Mill

RIVER BOLLIN

Bollin Mill

Brook St homes

Brook Street

Gothic style doorway Sunderland Street

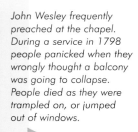

Culverted section of the Bollin under the station

Sluice-gate of the Dam Brook at Pickford Street

Mill workers' dwellings by the side of the river on Brook Street

Riverside walk back towards Macclesfield

Remains of the old Lower Heys Mill by the Bollin

Leather Mill built c1820 - note the privy linked to the chimney towards the left

The Globe company was the last cotton mill in Macclesfield and employed around 2000 workers

Lower Heys Mill (Globe cotton millweaving shed b1867)

RIVER BOLLIN

To Riverside Park

Site of former Hibel Road Railway Station and goods yard

HURDSFIELD ROAD

THE SILK ROAD

Leather Mill

Thorpe Street

Commercial Road

To Macclesfield town centre

Bollin clean-up

Following an epidemic of scarlet fever in June 1893, workmen began cleaning the Bollin. It followed a period of dry weather and reports of a stench from the river. The local hospital was full and all the local schools had to be closed for a month as precaution.

Left: Macclesfield Town Hall, Market Place

Below left: One of three Saxon pillars from Ridge Hall farm, now at West Park

Below right: Restored workers' homes built 1825 with top-floor garrets, on Paradise Street

Bottom left: Unitarian chapel built in 1690 following the Act of Toleration which allowed dissenting groups to have their own place of worship.

Bottom right: Macclesfield Sunday School, Roe Street, built 1813, where silk mill child workers were taught reading, writing and Christianity on their one day off. The site is now a silk museum and community centre.

Riverside Park

The 70 acre park stretches alongside the Bollin between Macclesfield and Prestbury. The land previously used for agricultural purposes is now an area of open countryside, wildflower meadows and woods. Since its opening as a riverside park, paths and seating areas have been made and trees, flowers and shrubs planted. Longhorn cattle introduced by the Bollin Valley Partnership help to maintain the wild flowers in the park. There is also a butterfly garden, bird feeding station, picnic areas and a visitor centre at Beechwood Mews.

The Bollin Valley Way, a 25-mile walkway to Partington, begins here, marked with the 'Birdman' carving by Alan Beirs.

Celtic burial

A Bronze Age urn was discovered at nearby Beech Hall School in 1960. Workman digging a trench for a swimming pool uncovered the remains of a two-year old child who had suffered from rickets. It is thought that the 1200BC clay urn had been buried here because of its position on a promontory overlooking the river Bollin.

Above: Longhorn cattle at Riverside. Right: Green veined white butterfly

PRESTBURY

Above: The bank building known as the Priest's House was probably built as two cottages in the 15th century. It is thought to have been a vicarage and that the priest delivered his sermons from the balcony and conducted marriage ceremonies here.

Below: Prestbury has won many civic awards

Prestbury

The village is renowned for having the rich and famous among its inhabitants, and for possessing one of the most picturesque main streets in Cheshire. In the central conservation area there are many fine old buildings to admire including Prestbury Hall, the Priest's House, the Bridge Hotel and St Peter's Church - one of the oldest in the country.

Prestbury's name is thought to have derived from 'Preosta burh', meaning priests' fortified enclosure. This would have been a secure base next to the river Bollin for the priests to move around the extensive parish. Until the building of a bridge in 1825, the Bollin had to be forded by Pearl Street to reach Butley. The village used to hold wakes and cattle fairs in the main street, and it has been a centre for silk weaving with a mill and weavers' cottages.

Above: The Legh Arms (left) dates back to 1580. It was a popular venue during the annual cattle fairs in April and October, and for parish tea parties. Windows were boarded up and railings erected during the fairs to prevent damage

Dr Mary Roberts

Above: Prestbury Mill and mill cottage

Below: The 1940 mill fire, believed to have been started by a worker's blow torch heating up the machinery while he was on the phone to a customer. Many businessmen on their way to the railway station stopped to help remove goods and materials from the mill - ruining their clothes in the process. Crowds watching the fire were seen to be holding umbrellas, not as protection from the rain but from the fire brigade's leaky hose pipes.

Jean Wright

Prestbury Mill

The old mill behind St Peter's Church is now the site of the Abbey Mill retirement homes which opened in 2002. There is a reference to a corn mill at Prestbury in 1268 when it belonged to St Werburgh's Abbey, which was later re-dedicated as Chester Cathedral. Throughout most of the nineteenth century and towards the 1920s, the Thompstone family were the millers and later, owners. John Thompstone was listed at the mill in 1848 and remained there until his death in 1883. It passed into the ownership of Isaac Thompstone and Co. corn merchants and millers, possibly a cousin of John. Isaac's son, Harold, was the last member of the family to own the mill. He died in France on active service in 1918, and the following year much of the milling equipment and cleaning machinery was auctioned.

The mill was taken over by Richard Wright, a grocer and corn dealer from Bollington, and the business continued with his sons Clifford and Leslie. But in March 1940, the historic old mill was severely damaged by fire. The blaze started soon after the mill engines had been switched on at 7.50am. The foreman heard a huge explosion, then saw fire breaking out on a ledge near an oil tank. Arriving employees helped to salvage as much corn and feeding stuffs as they could, along with furniture and the company's account books. The fire could be seen for miles around, with many watching from the adjoining churchyard. Although it was brought under control by 11am, the firm's principal, Isaac Wright, estimated 200 tonnes of corn and animal feed had been lost. The mill walls remained standing, and it was found that old grave stones, presumably brought from the nearby graveyard, had been used as flooring.

After the incident there were questions about the local auxiliary fire service being unable to tackle the blaze because they did not have enough equipment. There had also been a delay while the Macclesfield Volunteer Fire Brigade arrived and their efforts were hampered because the pumps were clogged with tons of corn which had fallen into the Bollin.

The mill was later rebuilt and sold by the Wrights to Hamlyn and Co., millers, in November 1946. By 1966, the old mill was due to be demolished to be replaced by a new extension. After Hamlyns closed, the property was used by a computer company and then JP Rose Garages. The site was sold to Bryant Homes in 1998 and work began on filling-in the old mill pool. Plans were submitted for retirement homes on the site in 2000 by English Courtyard Association, and the following year the mill was demolished.

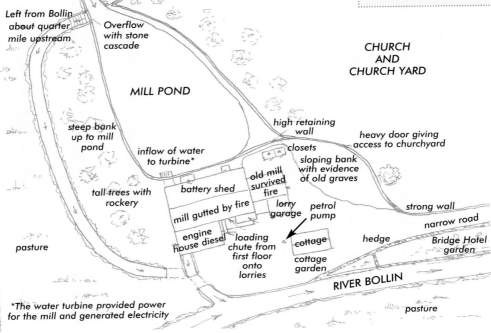

Drawing of Prestbury Mill by L Benson from boyhood memory 1928

Above: The Admiral Rodney Inn is named after George Rodney, god-son of King George I. He achieved success in battles against the French and Spanish fleets in the West Indies and Spain. Further along the street are the taller weavers' cottages. Weavers worked on the top floor away from the grime of the road.

Right top: Cottages, Pearl Street, built in 1686 by Roger Brooks. He and his future wife began work on their home before they were married, and used stone from the bed of the river Bollin. After his death the cottage was rented out at 1s 6d for many years.

Right below: Spectacular series of weirs on the Bollin, close to the centre of the village

Left: The river bed by the side of Bollin Grove is paved. It helped to reduce turbulence in the water to Butley corn mill which stood at the end of the Grove. The mill later changed use into a cotton factory and then silk weaving. The mill had closed by the end of the 19th century and the remaining part was demolished in 1964. Parts of the Bridge Hotel by the Bollin date back to 1626

Below: Spittle House, built by monks between 1300 and 1475 as an almshouse or hospital. The oldest 'elbow-cruck' section is still intact. In 1625 the owner of Spittle was hanged for murdering a local man. Another half-timbered building on the site was demolished in the 17th century for a brick-built house to the right of the old building.

Memorial to Reginald Legh, son of Robert Legh, Knight, who died in 1482

Chancel memorial to Robert and Matilda Downes. Robert of Pot Shrigley died in 1495.

St Peter's Church

There has been a place of worship here since Anglo-Saxon times. Work began on the present building about 1220 when it belonged to the Abbey of St Werburgh, Chester. The building was not fully completed until 1741 by Charles Legh with stone from the Kerridge quarries. Further alterations and extensions based on plans by Sir Gilbert Scott were carried out between 1879 and 1885.

The earliest inscribed monument in the church is to Reginald Legh who was involved in the building of the tower and the porch around 1480. Another memorial is to Sir Edward Warren of Poynton, shown in full armour, who died in 1558. He was in the party which went to Scotland in 1544 to demand the surrender of the infant Mary Queen of Scots, so that she could be married to Edward, the King's son.

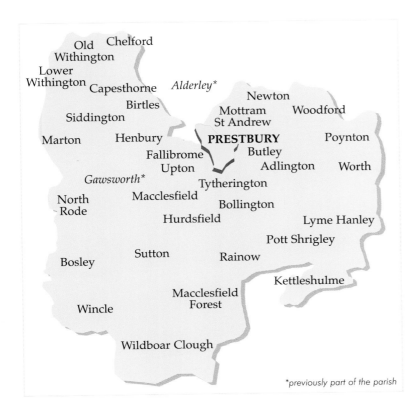

Old Withington
Chelford
Lower Withington
Capesthorne
*Alderley**
Birtles
Newton
Mottram St Andrew
Woodford
Siddington
Henbury
PRESTBURY
Poynton
Marton
Fallibrome
Butley
Upton
Adlington
Worth
*Gawsworth**
Tytherington
Macclesfield
North Rode
Bollington
Hurdsfield
Lyme Hanley
Pott Shrigley
Sutton
Rainow
Bosley
Kettleshulme
Wincle
Macclesfield Forest
Wildboar Clough

previously part of the parish

Left: Prestbury parish was 14 miles long and 10 miles wide, covering 33 townships. St Peter's was the mother church and the only one licensed to conduct marriage services until 1878. People used to wait at the old Unicorn Inn before the ceremony. Locals seeing the prospective brides there nicknamed it the 'joiners' shop'.

The Norman Chapel (see photo page 53) was used for worship until 1216. It would have replaced a timber-framed Saxon church in about 1175. The new stone building became too small for the large parish but, unusually, it was not incorporated into the new church.

The seven figures on the front of the chapel are thought to represent the Holy Trinity, the monarch (probably Richard I), a warrior, a priest and St Peter with the key.

A visiting historian in 1592 recorded that the chapel was in ruins and roofless. Sir William Meredith of Henbury had the building repaired in 1747 and in return, he and his family were granted the privilege of using it for private burials.

By 1828 the old chapel was used as a day school and Sunday school. The chapel began to decay again until the new vicar organised restoration work in 1953.

There is a brass plate inscription to Edward and Alice Newton of Butley who had seven sons and seven daughters. Their eldest son, Thomas, was a fine classical scholar and writer, and later became a master at Macclesfield Grammar School. The Legh family have held the manor of Prestbury since 1580, and within the Legh Chapel there is a monument to Charles Legh of Adlington Hall who died in 1781.

The church registers date back to the time of Elizabeth 1, and include an entry in 1630 of a boy being paid 10d to drive dogs out of the church, and in 1707 the costs of gunpowder and coal to celebrate what we know as 'Bonfire night'. A 1729 vestry meeting ordered that five shillings be paid for every fox killed in the parish.

The curfew bell rang daily from the time of Elizabeth 1 at 8pm. The pudden bell rang at noon, along with the early porridge bell and the pancake bell at 11am on Shrove Tuesday. The church bells rang out in joy in 1745 as the Duke of Cumberland's army passed through the village in the chase for the fleeing Jacobites.

St Peter's Church yard

Right: Known as the 'Saxon Cross', it was made from three fragments of stone found embedded in the church wall during restoration work in 1841. It is thought to date from the 9th or 10th century. Some believe it was part of a cross made in the 8th century by Saxon Christian converts.

Rathbone tomb

(**1** - large table tomb near gate) Maria Rathbone aged 8 died in 1821 after getting lost after leaving a shop at Henbury. She wandered through neighbouring villages but nobody helped her. She was still out on a December night during a snow storm. Her body was found in a field close to the Crown Inn at Peover, twenty-five days later.

(**2** - stone coffin) on the south side of tower is thought to have been for Vivian Davenport of Marton, Chief Forester of Macclesfield Forest and Grand Sergeant of the Macclesfield Hundred c1250. It was found beneath the basement of the outer wall in 1882.

Forester tomb

(**3** - tomb and sundial) William Wyatt of Adlington, a quarryman age 41, was shot while capturing two armed highwaymen at Shrigley in 1848. His brother was also wounded in the arm. A public collection raised £1000 for William's widow and children. His brother received £400, and £170 was given to the other quarrymen who had confronted the highwaymen. The robbers were hanged at Chester.

(**4** - table tomb, under tree) Thomas Rylance of Shrigley, Captain in the 43rd Light Infantry Regiment, set off for home from Gibraltar on 26 September 1823 on the brig Hope which is thought to have been destroyed by fire and never seen again.

(**5** - flat stone) William Davies age 17 of Prestbury who was killed by a fall from the rigging on board the ship Kenyon on a voyage to Calcutta November 1866.

(**6** - tomb) William Cawley in 1821 whose 'penmanship and drawing were unequalled'.

Wyatt sundial

(**7** - flat stone) July 1881, Benjamin Broadhurst age 62, served 24 years in the 6th Dragoon Guards and fought in the Crimea and Indian Mutiny. For the past 16 years he had been the Sergeant Major in the Earl of Chester's Yeomanry Cavalry.

(**8** - grave) 1932 James Hopwood, church organist with an inscription with a musical clef.

(**9** - flat stone) 1759 Paul Mason of Rainow, father and grandfather to 94 children

(**10** - Saxon cross) see facing page

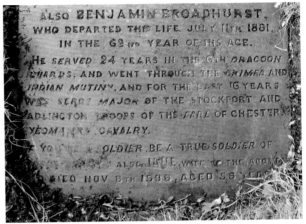

Broadhurst tomb

(**11** - tomb) James Pickford from Poynton, founder of the removal firm, buried here in 1768.

Among the other graves are those of **Thomas and Alice Broad** who lost nine of their children ranging from 11 months to 21 between 1787 and 1803. Alice died in 1825 age 66.

Thomas Bann who died age 105 in 1824.

Edward Green died from wounds sustained when trying to arrest Joseph Clarke of Kerridge End in 1750 for stealing deer. Green was the parish constable and stonemason. Clarke had previously killed one of the Pretender's Jacobite followers at Macclesfield in 1745 and was later caught and hanged at Chester.

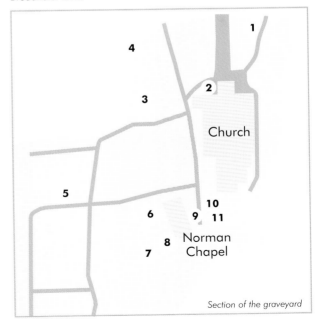

Section of the graveyard

Today, the hall is an eight-bedroomed mansion set in about one and a half acres, backing onto the golf course

Prestbury Hall

It is thought to have been built in the 15th century when Sir Richard Sutton was one of its earliest owners. Born here in 1460, he was a lawyer and became a Privy Counsellor in 1498. He co-founded Brasenose College, Oxford and a portrait of him in armour is to be seen at the college. He owned large tracts of land in Oxfordshire and Essex which he gave to the college. Sutton also contributed to Corpus Christie College where his coat of arms is over the gateway entrance. Sutton was a patron of the arts, paying for the publishing in 1519 of 'The Orchade of Syon', said to be a fine example of ancient English typography. King Henry VIII knighted him in 1522.

In 1790 Prestbury Hall was restored in the Georgian style, the frontage plastered, rooms added onto the garden side and the whole exterior whitewashed. James, the son of prosperous merchant and manufacturer Thomas Hope grew up here. He was born in 1801 at Stockport, attended Macclesfield Grammar School and went on to become one of the foremost physicians of his generation. His pioneering work in heart disease culminating, after many papers on the subject, with his 1831 book 'A Treatise on the Heart and Great Vessels' made him world-famous. For the next three years he taught and practised medicine in London, before completing a publication of anatomical drawings - a project he had begun at the start of his medical education in Edinburgh. In July 1840 he was elected a fellow of the London College of Physicians but his health suddenly deteriorated and he died of pulmonary consumption the following May, age 40.

John Lawton lived at the Hall for about twenty years before returning, amidst scenes of great local rejoicing, to the family seat at Lawton near Chester in 1860. By 1875 Prestbury Hall was described as '...quaint and picturesque.. and resembling a French chateau' because of a rounded turret added during the earlier alterations.

Silk manufacturer, Richardson Andrew, was the next occupant at Prestbury. He had silk mills at Newton Heath Manchester, Macclesfield and Leigh, and was a key supporter of William Cunliffe Brooks who was elected MP for Cheshire in 1869. Andrew died age 45 in 1879.

An advertisement to let the hall and grounds in 1882 described it as having twelve and a half acres with a further five hundred and eighty acres of adjoining land for shooting. There were vineries and green houses and stabling for four horses; the hall had eleven bedrooms, four reception rooms, butler's pantry and wash-house.

Thomas Gair Ashton, living at the hall by 1891, was Liberal MP for Hyde 1885-6, and South Bedfordshire from 1895 until his elevation to the peerage in 1909 when he became Lord Ashton of Hyde. He was born in Didsbury Manchester and was an East India merchant in the cotton trade. Ashton was a JP, a governor of Manchester University and on the Education Committee at Hyde. He was also a member of the group which set up Manchester Technical School which later developed into the College of Technology on Whitworth Street Manchester. Away from politics he was active in the family business of Ashton Brothers as well as being prominent in the civic development of Hyde where his family had originated.

The hall became a dower house to Adlington Hall and Mrs Legh died at Prestbury in 1901. Frank Donner, an export merchant listed at the hall in 1910, was a member of the firm Chamberlin Donner and Co and was actively interested in medical charities as well being the honorary secretary of Manchester Ear Hospital.

Cheshire Life

Top: The rounded turret extension
Above: Thomas Gair Ashton

Owners & occupiers

1810 - Thomas Hope, owned by Richard Legh

1837 - John Lawton, owned by Charles Richard Banastre Legh *(Lawton returned to his ancestral estate August 1860)*

1861 - Richardson Andrew

1882 - *Hall to let*

1883 - Robert Holliday

1886 - Joseph Farbridge Halliday

1891 - Thomas Gair Ashton

1901 - Death of Mrs Legh of Prestbury Hall 20 January

1902 - Burt Owen

1906 - Edward Mosley Owen

1910 - Frank Donner

1923 - Philip M Armitage

Col Armitage purchased the property from the Legh Estates April 1927

1940 - *Contents of hall put up for sale by Mrs Armitage*

1954 - Restored as a private residence by Victor Eva

Colonel Philip Armitage purchased the hall from the Legh estates in 1927. The grounds of the hall had been leased to Prestbury and Upton Golf Club in 1920. Mrs Armitage, who was a JP, had the contents of the hall auctioned in 1940.

The Hall, along with Collar House in Prestbury, was requisitioned by St Mary's Maternity Hospital for evacuated Manchester mothers (including the author's). The city centre hospital was considered at risk from enemy bombing and so they relocated to the countryside where mothers could give birth in relative peace and security. The outbuildings and stables were utilised by the ARP, Home Guard, Boy and Girl Scouts and as a waste paper collection point.

Proposals to open a maternity hospital at Prestbury Hall were made in late 1940, but it was not until serious bomb damage in Merseyside in May the following year that the authorities hurriedly opened the unit with volunteers and staff from St Mary's. The 22 beds at the hall continued to be used until 1953 because of the shortage of beds and the post-war baby boom. In 1946 the North Western Bus Company was given permission to run a service for visitors to the hall and Collar House from Manchester for the one-hour visiting times on Wednesdays, Saturdays and Sundays. Mothers were kept at the hospital for about two weeks, with the first five days in bed. They only saw their babies at feeding time because they were looked after by the midwives. Births increased in Manchester from 10,276 in 1941 to about 12,700 in 1944.

Victor and Elsie Eva at the hall in 1960

Cheshire Life

It closed as a maternity hospital in 1951 and became a nurses home for a year. The hall remained empty for several years until it was bought by Victor Eva, chairman of Eva Industries Ltd. He had first noticed and admired the hall in the 1930s as he was playing golf on its former grounds. Its use as a maternity hospital had left its mark in the hall with partitions installed to divide up the large rooms, and damaged cornices. When Mr and Mrs Eva took ownership in 1956, they had to deal with dry and wet rot, flooded cellars and serious roofing problems before they could complete substantial renovations. Workmen uncovered original stone mullioned window and door frames.

Collar House

Today it is known as Prestbury Beaumont Care Home, but the property previously called Collar House dates back to about 1780 when it was owned by the Hordern family. It was originally a farm house, then converted into a gentleman's residence c1861 with the arrival of Manchester merchant Robert Hervey - a dealer in paints, glue and dyes. After his death in 1873, it became the home of David Chadwick, who was described as 'one of the fathers of accountancy' because of his involvement in helping to reorganise or rescue failing companies. Chadwick was MP for Macclesfield and generously paid for the building of the library and its 7000 books in 1875.

Part of the house used as a war-time maternity home

Swinton-born cotton manufacturer Gerald Peel lived here between 1880 and 1888 and was a bell ringer at the parish church. Later he went to live in Worsley and became widely known for his public and philanthropic work. As well as being a magistrate, he was a governor of Manchester Children's Hospital, president of the Manchester Blind Aid Society, and the Swinton and Pendlebury Civic Guild of Help.

Isaac Crewdson Waterhouse, who lived at Collar House for 26 years, was a partner at Horrocks, Crewdson and Co. Piccadilly, Manchester. The company also had the largest cotton shed in the world at Moses Gate, Preston. The family were noted for the lavish parties held at the house which had a ballroom and organ, with the guests arriving by carriage. Waterhouse generously donated to local causes, and was responsible for the building of Prestbury Village Club in 1907 as an alternative to the local pubs. He collapsed and died while playing golf at Poole in 1913. His cousin, Alfred, was the great architect, and another cousin, Edwin, helped found the accountancy firm Price Waterhouse Cooper.

Reginald Moseley, who lived at Collar House from 1914, was chairman of the family firm David Moseley and Sons, india rubber manufacturers based at the Chapel Fields works in Ardwick Manchester. They were also pioneering producers of telephone equipment and installed the first private line between two business premises in the city centre. The company was one of the largest rubber manufacturers in the North West.

In about 1937, Moseley went to live near Menai Bridge, North Wales where he had moorings and a yacht, and died there in 1957.

Many people remember Collar House as a war-time and post-war maternity home for St Mary's Hospital, Manchester. St Mary's had originally planned to evacuate expectant mothers to Blackpool and transferred fifty staff with their equipment there, but it soon became obvious that most of the mothers did not want to travel so far.

The property was leased to St Mary's Hospital in 1939 at an annual rent of £310. The 75-acre estate at Prestbury with gardens, glasshouses and views over Cheshire opened in December 1939. At this time the head gardener was Jonathan Beresford, a Fellow of the Royal Horticultural Society and gardening correspondent for the Manchester Evening News, writing over 3000 articles. He gave talks on improving allotments and won many horticultural prizes.

Owners & occupiers

1780 - 1859 - Hordern family, owners

1810 - Laurence Gaskell

1859 - Robert Hervey

1874 - David Chadwick, tenant

1880 - Gerald Peel

1888 - Isaac Waterhouse

1914 - Reginald Moseley

1939 - 1952 St Mary's Hospital

1988 - Beaumont Care

Collar House had its own water and electrical supplies and laundry. There were labour wards, nurseries, a dispensary and an operating theatre. The hospital had forty-five beds and accommodation for the thirty staff, and around seven thousand babies were born there. Ambulances took the mothers-to-be from St Mary's to Collar House and the hall at Prestbury.

Later extension at the care home

The matron only allowed doctors to drive to the front door, everyone else including expectant mothers had to make their own way or be carried up the slope to the house. In 1946, the hospital bought Collar House for £9,750. 800 cases a year were dealt with at a cost of about £12,732. Income from private patients raised £4,500.

It became a post-operative and convalescent home in 1953 for patients from Macclesfield Infirmary and West Park Hospital. There used to be open fires in every room which the porters had to keep alight. Collar House closed in 1984, and the patients were transferred to new premises on Victoria Road. Beaumont acquired the property in 1988 and built extensions to the house, while demolishing the old kitchen block and several cottages close by.

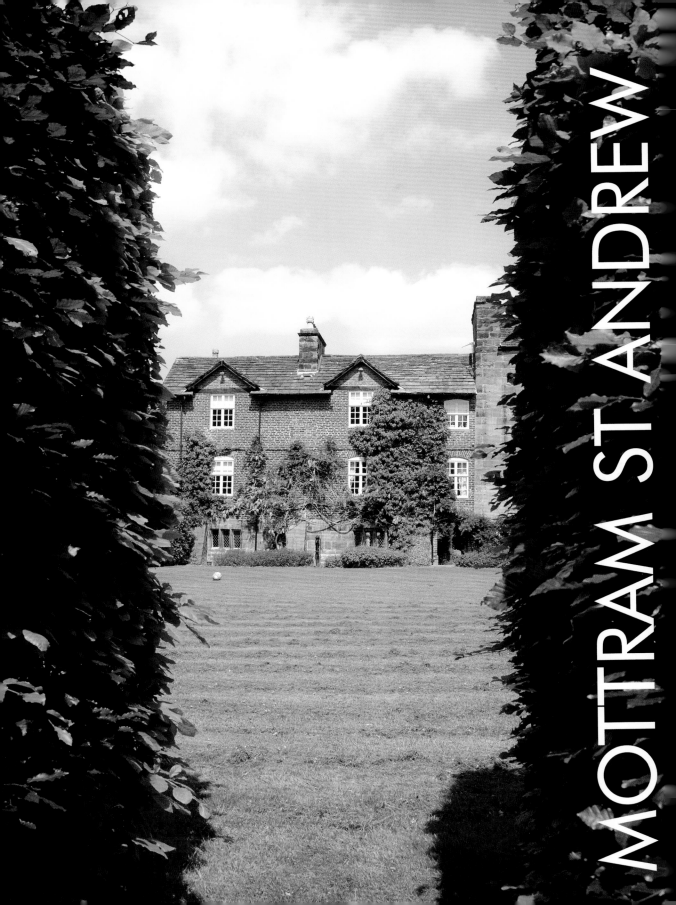

MOTTRAM ST ANDREW

Previous page: Mottram Old Hall

Right: Mottram Cross in its original position. It has a Medieval base with a 19th century shaft and head with the arms of the Wright family and the date of its restoration. The previous site of the cross is marked by a pavement plaque.

This was the site of a Saxon cross and may have marked the old boundary of Macclesfield Forest.

The old village school was built by the Wrights close to the cross, and attended by a hundred children. In 1868 the villagers were in dispute with the Wrights over ownership of the school. Later it was demolished and a new council school was built in the village.

Below: The Bollin near Mill farm on Mill Lane

70

Above: The Bollin near Mottram Wood

Left: The original Legh Old Hall was built in the 1290s and the remains used to build the present cottage.

The adjacent New Hall (formerly known as Lee Hall) was built in 1701 with later Victorian extensions.

In the early 1900s it was the home of Mrs Walter Greg who organised many events such as Christmas parties and summer trips for the village. A room at the hall was used for plays and readings for the villagers. She also organised a clothing club, a Band of Hope and classes for children. Women of the village always received a gift from her when they married.

Left: Site of the moated 13th century manor house of William de Foxtwist. The house was taken down in 1357, and a new structure built. It passed into the ownership of the Leghs of Adlington and by the 17th century a cottage stood on the site. This was demolished around 1920.

Mottram Old Hall

The Motterum family were lords of the manor in the 12th century. Several of them held the prestigious title of Bailiff of the Forest. Roger de Mottram fought for the Black Prince in the Battle of Poitiers in 1356. Title to the land passed by marriage to the Calveley family and they built the present semi-fortified manor house with a moat on three sides. The manor remained in the possession of the Calveleys for around 300 years, after which it was bought by Nathaniel Booth and then Richard Crooke of Macclesfield in 1716. Crooke died without direct descendants and the manor was bought by William Wright in 1738. After the building of the new hall, the old hall became the land agent's house.

Below: Tractarian and memorial to Rev Henry Wright, St Peter's Church Stockport

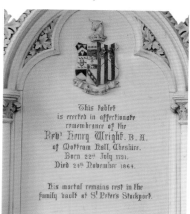

Mottram Hall

The new hall was built in about 1752 by wealthy landowner William Wright of Offerton for his son, Randal. But Wright's son died when he was twenty-one and never lived there. William's six other children also expired before reaching the age of twenty and the distraught father erected a monument to their memory in 1756 at St Mary's Church, Stockport. William's own memorial at the church reads 'a life of Seventy-three years, embittered with Pain and Trouble'. He paid for the building of St Peter's Church which was consecrated in 1768 and endowed it with income from land at Mottram. The ancestors of the Wrights of Mottram and Offerton originated from Nantwich at the time of Edward IV.

The Wright family strictly observed the Sabbath, and tenants were expected to attend the service in the chapel at the hall conducted by the resident minister. Servants would walk in procession to church, led by the butlers and footmen with the maids and others behind.

Ownership of the hall passed through the Wright family in 1842 to Rev Henry Wright the incumbent of St Peter's, Stockport. His daughter Julia Catherine, was a member there and presented a Tractarian to the living in 1787. She later converted to Catholicism and gave a crucifix, seen next to the pulpit, to the church as a farewell gift.

Her husband, James Frederick Darley Street, changed his surname to Wright in order to inherit the estate. Born in Gibraltar, he became a captain in Royal Artillery and was a magistrate at the Macclesfield Petty Sessions.

Julia Catherine, along with other Cheshire landlords in 1899, closed the local inn, 'The Bull's Head' to deter Sunday visitors to her park who were trespassing and causing damage. She was described, when she died in 1916 aged 88, as one of Cheshire's biggest landowners with estates at Mottram St Andrew, Handforth, Horwich, Bolton and Leamington.

Julia Catherine's daughter, Julia Mary, married Edward Curteis JP of Leamington Spa, who was a captain with the 2nd Cheshire Regiment and served in Africa. He had taken part in the expedition to Griqualand West in 1875 to quell the revolt against British rule by white diamond miners known as 'diggers'. He resigned from the army to marry. He played cricket for Kent CC and the MCC in 1877. He died age 48 in 1902 after a lengthy illness.

Above: Crucifix given by Julia Wright to St Peter's Stockport

Below: Oak tree at Mottram Hall, thought to be one of the oldest trees in the Bollin Valley, dating back to c1600

75

Their son Edward Lawrence, who was heir to the extensive family estates, was convicted for driving offences on eight occasions. In the last case, in July 1908, he had been found guilty in Nottingham of driving on the wrong side of the road, and going at a dangerous speed. In view of his previous record, he was fined the extreme penalty of £20, together with £3 19s costs and his licence was suspended for twelve months. In previous cases he had been accused of speeding at Cheadle, Hazel Grove, Wilmslow, and Knutsford during a return trip from Blackpool motor races.

The following February, he died at Mottram Hall age 23. He was an enthusiastic motorist and a member of the AA - an organisation formed to warn their members of oncoming police speed traps. The previous day he had been to the Manchester motor show and returned around midnight. When his footman came to wake him at 8.30 the next morning, as instructed, he saw that Edward looked pale and had breathing difficulties. By the bed was a glass of dark liquid which the servant had noticed before over the previous weeks.

A doctor was called, but despite efforts of resuscitation, Edward died around noon. He had previously mentioned to staff that he had difficulty getting to sleep, but was still waking early.

At the Coroner's inquest it was established that Edward had died from an overdose of laudanum - a liquid form of opium, which he had taken to get to sleep. Mysteriously, there was no bottle at the scene, and therefore no evidence as to where he had obtained it. The Coroner questioned why Curteis had not consulted the doctor about his problem. Curteis seemed happy and healthy when he returned from Manchester and had not shown

Wright family grave at St Peter's Church, Stockport

any desire to take his own life, and a verdict of 'death by misadventure' was recorded.

Walter Pownall moved from Whalley Range Manchester to the hall about 1916. He and his brother Harold set up the company W & H Pownall Ltd, garment manufacturers. They moved from premises near Whitworth Street to a new factory known as the Daisy Bank Works at Stockport Road Longsight, Manchester in 1904. There were about 2000 employees, and 'Daisy Make' was the brand name for their products.

Cinnabar moths at Mottram

18th century horse-drawn carriage wheel wash

Half of the works were destroyed by fire in 1928 but it had been rebuilt and, in newspaper advertising, Pownall's highlighted the improved safety features and working conditions. However, the company had already been fined in 1925 by magistrates for failure to rectify plumes of black smoke billowing from its chimney. There had been several complaints and forty residents had signed a petition about the nuisance.

Swan Mussel, Mottram Hall pond

Then, in 1929, Pownalls were again summoned to court over 165 contraventions of the Factories and Workshops Act. Offences included: illegal shift-working, unfenced machinery, locked outer doors, failing to register accidents, working excessive hours, and employing young people without a medical certificate. It was pointed out that during the 1928 fire, around 100 female workers had been padlocked in the factory and had to be rescued by the police breaking down a door. Pownall's were fined a total of £566.

Pownall's works in Manchester

The following year two teenage boys died in a fire at the works. The blaze started in a wooden shed known as the 'fluff-box' and it was thought that one youth had locked himself in and the other had died trying to rescue him. There was a further fire at the works in 1934 and another in 1940 which was started by a disgruntled former employee.

Dining room

Inner hall

During the last World War, the works were used by the Royal Army Pay Corps to administer officers' pay, including that of Field Marshall Montgomery. It has been suggested that the works would have been the Gestapo headquarters for Manchester if the enemy had invaded Britain.

In November 1938, Walter Pownall put Mottram Hall up for sale, announcing he was going to live in the south of England. His plans seemed to have changed because his next address was listed at Burlington Road Buxton. The following year, he had to go to the House of Lords to petition for a Bill which released him from the patronage of St Peter's Church Stockport and the right to select the minister. This right had been endowed with the ownership of Mottram Hall and the manor since 1768. Pownall died in December 1940 aged 64, in the Private Patients' Home at Manchester Royal Infirmary following illness after an accident.

The hall and 130 acres of park land were purchased in 1939 by the Manchester electrical engineering company Ferguson Palin Ltd, Openshaw as a country guest house and welfare centre for their 2000 employees and families. The hall was completely refurbished with accommodation for 100 guests and officially opened in April 1940. The dining room wood panelling came from the nearby Mottram Old Hall, and some of the rooms had 'Adam period' ceilings. There was also a billiard room, writing room and a large assembly room. Guests could stay for weekends or longer at 'moderate cost' with managers and shop floor workers mingling together. By 1943 about 1800 employees had been to stay at the guest house.

Housekeeper's room

The owners also made provision for the hall to be used by on-leave service men and women during war time. A programme of arts, sporting and leisure activities was laid on.

The UCP and Stanneylands catering group re-opened Mottram Hall as a hotel and restaurant in 1972, then in 1977 it was purchased by the Greenall's group and has become part of the De Vere Hotels group. Within the extensive grounds there is a championship golf course, an FA accredited pitch and woodland and river walks.

WILMSLOW

*Previous page: Weir
at Wilmslow Park*

*This page and opposite:
the Bollin Valley Way
near Dean Row*

Emperor dragonfly

The Bollin near Vardon Bridge which took two years to rebuild being completed in 1786.

ALAN TURING
1912 - 1954
Founder of computer science
and cryptographer, whose work
was key to breaking the
wartime Enigma codes,
lived and died here.

Alan Turing, one of Britain's greatest computer scientists and mathematicians, moved to Adlington Road, Wilmslow in 1950. The next year a burglary here set up a train of events which eventually led to medical treatment for his homosexuality. He continued at Manchester University but later committed suicide.

17th century Unitarian Chapel at Dean Row, similar in design to those at Knutsford and Macclesfield. Members of the Greg mill family are buried here.

Wilmslow Park

The Longhorn herd at Wilmslow Park and also at Riverside Park, Macclesfield were once the most popular cattle in the county. They were valued for providing meat for the growing populations in the industrial towns; however it had, until recently, become a rare breed. Today they are regarded by chefs for their high quality and were selected by the Bollin Valley Partnership, both to promote the breed, and because they are hardy and docile in nature.

It is unusual to see rare breeds so close to the towns, and their grazing helps to conserve the flower-rich meadows. During the winter they are housed at Oakwood Farm, Styal so that they don't churn up the fields during bad weather. New-born calves can be sponsored, named and access given to track their progress.

Longhorn cattle

St Bartholomew's Church

Top: Humphrey Newton tomb
Above: Bell tower

Wilmslow Parish Church

There has been a church on this site since the 13th century on the banks of the Bollin built by Sir Richard Fitton who held the manor of Bolyn. The present St Bartholomew's was erected mainly between 1517 and 1537, with restoration taking place from 1861 to 1863. The church had been in poor condition and the grounds were water-logged. Floorboards had rotted away and fallen into the crypt below, and the minister stood on a box to prevent his feet from getting wet. During the latter alterations, old fittings, oak pews and the 1543 altar tomb of George Booth were removed. Fortunately the 16th-century side chapel screens survived because there were not enough funds to remove them.

William Gladstone, the future British Prime Minister, came to Wilmslow in 1828 to be tutored by the Rector JM Turner. He had left Eton and went on to Oxford in the autumn of that year. The Rev Turner helped to improve Gladstone's mathematics skills before going on to be Bishop of Calcutta.

The bell tower contains a 1657 Sanctus bell and six bells dating from 1733. Benefactors to the poor are listed, and two tablets indicate repairs in 1658 and 1810. There is a memorial to thirteen-year old John Hunt who was overcome by the noise of the bells in 1767 after hiding in the ringing chamber. Locals used to claim that 'the Wilmslow bells ring themselves', which was true because the Bell family were bell ringers here.

Much of the original 16th-century woodwork of the church roof has survived, with emblems of the Honford family of Handforth Hall but also a small ceiling image of either the devil or possibly a 'green man'. The effigies of Humphrey Newton (1466-1560) and his wife Ellen are to be seen in the Jesus Chapel. His head rests on three barrels whilst her pillow is a wheatsheaf, the Fitton family symbol. Henry Trafford, the rector who rebuilt the church, was buried here in 1537 during the reign of Henry VIII.

This part of the church used to be known as the Trafford Chapel because it was built at the expense of the Trafford family in about 1520. They inherited the right to appoint the rector about a hundred years previously, when the parish had been split into two manors, following the death of Richard Venables. He had been the heir to the estate but drowned in the River Bollin.

The 1460 memorial to Sir Robert Del Bouthe 'knight, formerly Lord of Bolyn, Thoneton and Dunham' and his wife Douce on the floor of the Prescott Chapel is said to be the oldest brass of its kind in Cheshire. They were married when they were children but enjoyed a long happy life together. The 16th-century parish chest made from a single piece of oak used to contain the parish register and other documents. Records show that fourpence was paid for killing urchins - hedgehogs - and twopence for powder and shot to dispatch the nuisance pigeons from the church.

Pews and panelling in the Hawthorne Chapel date back to the 18th century. Below is the sealed-off vault of the Leigh family, rediscovered in the 1980s. The organ was restored in 1931 with a woodwork case by master carpenter James Brown from Mobberley, in memory of his wife. The carvings show her interest in needlework, with scissors, and the tools of his trade - a hammer and chisel.

The small crypt chapel built in about 1300, is the oldest part of the church. It was restored in 1979 through a gift from the Lebanese Consul in Manchester and his children in memory of his wife. There are three glass panels here with the text 'Peace I give unto you' engraved in English, Arabic and Hebrew.

In the 18th century, William Bower built a cotton mill next to the Bollin on Mill Street by the Church. He used coal gas to light his mill and sold it to the public at 4p per light for a week's use. The mill was bought in 1857 by the owner of Bollin Manor and demolished so that the area remained residential.

Top: Mysterious face on roof boss
Above: Carving by local carpenter
Below: Crypt chapel

The Cemetery of St Bartholomew's

By WILMSLOW COMMUNITY ARCHAEOLOGY GROUP

The cemetery is the result of over a thousand years of history and numerous extensions. Until the mid l9th-century it was a small rounded enclosure dominated by the parish church, flanked by the old London Road, the Bollin crossing and a footpath known as the Steps **(1)**, leading to the tower of the church.

The limited size of the cemetery led to the use of grave markers and memorials for only the richer members of the parish. The earliest stone is that of the Dale family, in the shadow of the tower, and dates back to 1596 **(2)**. Many of the 17th and early 18th-century memorials were moved in the 20th century into the Prescott Chapel. Most of the stones represent the large landowning and tithing families of Wilmslow parish, including the Ward family **(3)**, yeomen in Wilmslow, Aldermen from Stockport, the Bowers (18th-century Wilmslow industrialists **(4)** - a generation before Samuel Greg), as well as the residents of some of the large houses such as the Worralls from Pownall Hall.

One of them - Captain Worrall **(5)**, was celebrated until the late 19th-century as the man who captured the French royal standard during one of Marlborough's battles. It made Wilmslow for a short time a star attraction in the early Baedecker's travel guides.

Many of these early graves have now only survived as the flat stones in the latest reincarnation of the 'the steps', now a footpath through the cemetery. Only two of the chests and altartombs **(6&7)** remain.

Above top: Interesting inscription
Above: St Bartholomew

Until the mid-18th century, the less well-off Wilmslow people were interred in temporary graves before having their bones transferred to a communal charnel house under the east end of the church. By the middle of the 19th-century the rapid growth of Wilmslow brought demands to extend the cemetery, while the continuing river erosion of the Bollin led to fears for the safety of the church building and surrounding properties. In 1862, the river was moved nearly 20 metres to the west of its former bed, with other properties removed.

From the 1860s onwards graves were available to all members of the church and in the 1880s people of other congregations were buried here, including Methodist and Presbyterian ministers. As a result, the churchyard includes all members of society, from the graves of the

burial club of Greg's Styal Mill, to those of the artisans of Wilmslow. The more affluent, both the families of the old landowners as well as the newly-arrived Manchester merchants and weavers, had more sumptuous graves with inlaid lettering, ornate carvings, and high crosses **(8)**.

Amongst the 'residents' are the Jennison family, who founded the Belle Vue show-ground **(9)**, as well as a Handforth police-man **(10)**, and the lady owners of a 19th century sweet shop in Fulshaw **(11)**. Some of the graves recall accidents in the area, such as the boy who drowned in the Bollin **(12)**, victims of the Gas Works accident **(13)** and a railway employee who died after being hit by a train **(14)**.

The church has surprising carvings ranging from 'green men' on the wall above the door of the church tower **(15)**, to the faces of a bishop and a middle-aged bald man complete with wrinkles, possibly portraying the various members of the medieval congregation, above the south window **(16)**. A fine 19th-century statue of St Bartholomew stands above the church door **(17)**, while the empty niches on the tower are a reminder of the medieval statues removed during the Reformation **(18)**.

About thirty years ago a large area of the cemetery was cleared and allowed to revert to nature and many of the older stones were either relocated or removed. There is a programme under way to record the surviving stones and research their importance.

Left: A wealthy person's grave
Below: Bald man, south window
Bottom: Green man over the tower door

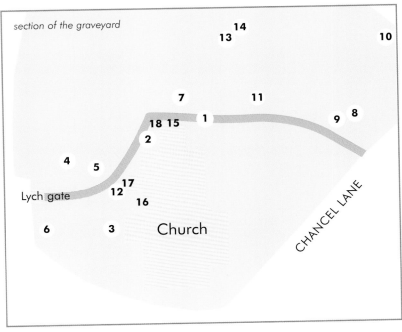

section of the graveyard

Lych gate

Church

CHANCEL LANE

Above: Bollin corn mill, on left, at Wilmslow
Below: The present day site

Bollin Corn Mill

The corn mill is referred to in 1249, when it was owned by the lord of the manor of 'Le Bolyn' - Sir Richard Fitton. The original mill may have been on the banks of the river with a water-wheel controlled by the flow of the river. Later mills here have utilised a controlled water supply from the Bollin using dams and sluice gates. Ownership of the area passed from the Fittons to the Venables, the Booths and to the Earls of Stamford, who sold off most of the Wilmslow estate in the 1850s.

The mill was destroyed by fire in November 1871. Passers-by returning from Stockport around 2.30am saw flames coming from the mill. They woke up the miller, Edwin Plant, who lived in the adjoining mill house, but were unable to save most of the corn, flour and Indian corn. Damage to the stock, floor, roofing and machinery was estimated at about £1000. Only the stables survived undamaged and were later converted into cottages. Locals noted that despite the area being the home of many affluent Manchester merchants, the nearest fire engines were stationed many miles away at Macclesfield and Stockport. Plant had checked the mill at 11pm the previous evening before he went to bed because he thought he had heard the sound of fireworks nearby.

The mill re-opened in about 1875 when the new miller, William Henry Coppock, advertised for a millworker. William Kitchen took over the mill in 1887. He lived next door to the mill at Prescot House and was the eldest son of a miller and corn merchant from Stockport.

William was also a director, then chairman, of the Wilmslow Gas Company, and a director of the Reddish Cemetery company. He was a member of the local Literary Institute and, for many years, a warden at the parish church. He bought the mill from the Prescot estate about 1920 and took an active part in the business right up to his death in 1932 at the age of 81.

Mr J Higginson worked at the mill from 1919 when he worked from 7am to 7pm for a wage of £3. At that time there were four people working in the mill and another four outside. The firm also had six horses. Robert Kitchen, who took over the mill after his father's death, was a familiar sight in the district on his business round, riding in a dog cart pulled by a lively horse. In 1949, owing to ill-health and declining business, he retired and sold the property to Gibson's builders. The mill wheel, with a triple row of wooden spokes mounted on an iron shaft with iron rims and wooden buckets, was removed about 1955.

Millers:

1786 - Joanathan Roylance

1799 - John Hatton

1818-20 - Edmund Hatton,

1823 - Thomas Walker

1837 - Owned by Earl of Stamford, John Pickford, occupier: John Handford(th)

1857 - William Mottram

1871 - Edwin Plant

1878 - William Henry Coppock

1881 - No mention of mill, but Richard Halliwell, corn miller, living nearby on Bollin Walk

1891 - William Kitchen

1932 - Robert Kitchen

Bollin Old Hall used to be situated close by, on the site of the railway arches. It was the manor house of the Venables family who owned the Bollin estate. (see Wilmslow Church) It was said to be a substantial brick building with dovecotes in the grounds, and extensive gardens. It had been likened by one local as similar to the timber-framed Chorley Hall.

During the demolition of the hall in 1842, a gold dessert spoon was found which reflected the wealth of those who lived there. It was once the practice for invited guests to bring their own cutlery made out of a metal which reflected their social standing.

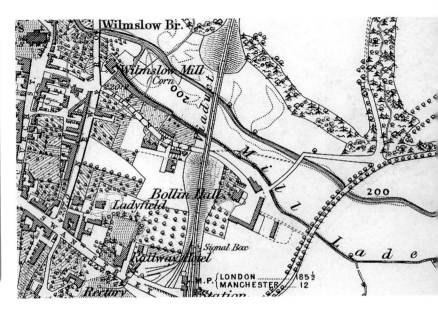

'Carrs' is a Norse word meaning meadow recovered from bog. It was once pasture land for the villagers.

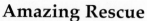

Pownall bridge, built 1820

Amazing Rescue

In January 1922, a small child fell into the Bollin at Wilmslow and was carried by the heavy current down the river for a quarter of a mile. The youngster had floated on its back before being rescued by H Morgan who lived on the banks of the Bollin. The child was given artificial respiration before regaining consciousness. Morgan had rescued another child just yards from the same spot a few years earlier.

The Carrs

A popular stretch of open land by the Bollin comprised of part of the Henry Boddington's Pownall Hall estate acquired in 1935, land known as 'Black Butts' purchased by the local authority in the 1930s, and a piece of the Greg property added in the 1960s. Since then work has taken place to repair the river banks, and a children's playground, bowling green and tennis courts have been installed. The Friends of the Carrs Group is active with other agencies to improve facilities and to combat the growing problem of alien species such as Himalayan Balsam.

Henry Boddington of Pownall Hall built the small private chapel overlooking the Carrs using discarded stone from the old parish church tower, and other local churches. It was dedicated to St Olaf, a Viking chieftain who was converted to Christianity in England and then returned to Norway where he became king. He converted the people to his faith but was later killed in battle, and became a national hero. The chapel had a frieze showing Olaf's battles and scenes from his life and death, and there was a pulpit, organ, altar table and a tower with a spiral staircase. There were many curious carvings both inside and outside the chapel by the sculptor JJ Millson. Over the years, the chapel was badly vandalised and by 1949 it had been largely demolished. Only a few stones remain today, and nearby there is an inscription on a boulder which describes how Henry Boddington planted an acorn which grew into the great oak tree standing beside the stone.

Above top: The Boddington Arch at the entrance to the Carrs

Above right: The stone near the oak grown by Henry Boddington

Left top and below left: St Olaf's Chapel

Right and below: The ruins of St Olaf's Chapel

Carr Mill

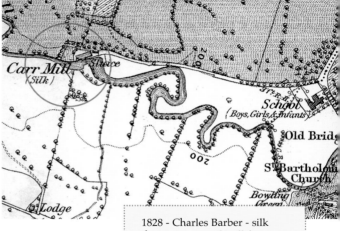

Originally a cotton mill owned and occupied by John Bower, but by 1828 it was being worked by Charles Barber, a silk throwster. Bower was made bankrupt in 1832 and the mill was sold. In 1841 it was owned jointly by the Earl of Stamford, Catherine Royle and Charles Barber. Later it became known as 'Barber's Mill' and in 1851 he employed 12 men, 18 women, 20 boys and 30 girls. By 1871 his nephew Charles ran the mill. The 1873 OS map refers to it as 'Carr Mill' and in 1878 the silk mill was operated by Burrowes and Forest. The 1896 directory lists a change of manufacture at the mill, with fustian cutter Ernest Platt in occupation.

The Wilmslow Laundry opened here in 1903 and claimed to be one of the most modern works of its kind, with the latest English and American washing machines and hydro-extractors, but completing the most delicate work by hand. Company vans brought the work in from around Greater Manchester. Heavy rains in August 1910 caused the River Bollin to flood and cause problems at the laundry for the second time in weeks.

In July 1915 a stack of coal and coke was discovered to be on fire in the early hours. Thirty laundry girls arriving for work quickly formed a line between the works and the river Bollin to pass buckets of water to put out the fire. A carpet cleaning shed was destroyed along with two vans.

There was another fire at the mill, then used as a gelatine works, in October 1923. By this time the premises had been used for various businesses and had been extensively renovated 18 months previously by the owner Henry Boddington, with a new roof and replacement windows. On the outside of the building it read 'The Calico Printers Association' but they never took possession. The fire had quickly taken hold in the early evening and by sunset, watched by large crowds, it had completely gutted the building, causing many thousands of pounds of damage. The fire was so fierce that even the waters of the Bollin were warm.

1828 - Charles Barber - silk throwster, rented mill from John Bower

1837 - Co-owned by Charles Barber, Earl of Stamford and Catherine Royle

1851 - Barber employing 12 men, 18 women, 20 boys and 30 girls.

1871 - Charles Barber's nephew of the same name in charge

1873 - OS map known as 'Carr Mill'

1878 - Burrowes and Forrest, silk throwsters

1881 - Christopher Brooks living at Silk Mill Cottage, employing 47 women, 34 boys and 7 men

1896 - Ernest Platt, fustian cutter

1903 - Wilmslow Laundry

Century Guild metalwork at the entrance

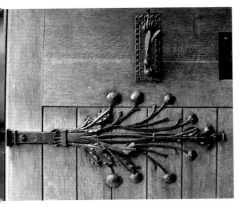

Pownall Hall

Today it is a private school but it was once a 148-acre estate with a farm, dower house, parkland and woods by the Bollin. The original hall was built by Richard de Pounale, a farmer, in 1297 and became the country seat of the Pownall family until 1328. It then passed into the ownership of the Fitton, Newton and Mainwaring families.

It was put up for sale in 1800 with suggested use, either for a gentleman's family or as a boarding school for young ladies. In about 1810 it was in use as a school. In 1817 the hall was bought by John Worrall but it was demolished and rebuilt in about 1833 by its new owner James Pownall, a Liverpool merchant, who claimed to be a descendant of the original family. Pownall also donated a new organ to the Parish Church in about 1840.

Pownall Hall was auctioned in 1853, and the next occupants were Edward Marsland, Mayor of Stockport, and magistrate, followed by Hugh Shaw, a cotton spinner and farmer, who died in 1862 age 71. Thomas Hobson, a Manchester cotton merchant, bought the hall in 1869 and made improvements. In his younger days he had made a vow of celibacy with his brother, John, but he later married and the two brothers never saw each other again. Thomas had a disagree-ment with the Rector at the Parish Church, where he was a church-

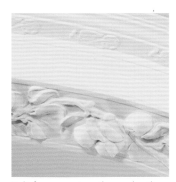

Relief ornament on the oval ceiling moulding in the former dining room

Exterior fitting by the front entrance

warden, regarding the collection of money for the poor, and began his own services at the hall, but this was stopped by an injunction. His wife ran a soup kitchen for the needy in the town, and his children and their friends enjoyed sailing a boat on the Bollin. His business failed with debts of nearly £22,000 in March 1886 and he died the following month.

The interior of the house underwent significant change in 1886 after it was bought by Henry Boddington, the son of the owner of the Manchester brewery at Strangeways. Up to that time he had been living in a flat above the business. Henry transformed the house into the newly-emerging Arts and Crafts style. The best designers and craftspeople were brought in to produce stained glass windows, furniture, fabrics and panelling. The Century Guild of Artists, an organisation promoting equality between artists and craftsmen, was commissioned to design the dining room and drawing room, and also furnish the other rooms, each with distinctive fittings and features such as ornamental metal work. Discarded oak panels from churches around Derbyshire and North Wales costing £20,000 were utilised, and the crests of previous families at Pownall featured in the rooms. Boddington built a gallery at the back of the house for his paintings, which included many of the works of Ford Madox Brown, and a collection of early keyboard instruments. It was also the place for the family to perform plays.

The library in 1891

'Atlantes' by Benjamin Creswick in the former dining roo

The staircase and interiors were designed by architects Ball and Elce

Fireplace carving of the Norse days of the week, in the entrance hall

Lecturn in the entrance hall

Entrance hall with an oak-beamed ceiling, polished wooden panelling and half timbering

Section of window depicting Dante and Chaucer by Morris & Co

Scenes from 'As You Like It' by Manchester artist John Dawson Watson

Eurydice and Orpheus

St Michael and fruit tree by Shrigley and Hunt

Mural of a medieval procession in the former nursery hall by JD Watson

Godesses Juno and Latona

*Nursery rhyme on stained glass
in the former school room*

*Above: One of a series of six
figures in the former dining room*

*Left: West end of the hall, with
the former library bay*

Owners & occupiers

1817 - John Worrall

1833 - James Pownall

1850 - Peter Pownall
and Edward Marsland,
Borough magistrate

1853 - *For sale by auction
30th August*

1857 - Hugh Shaw,
cotton spinner and farmer

1862 - *Contents of hall
auctioned 3-5th November*

1864 - Thomas Hobson,
cotton merchant

1886 - Henry Boddington

1894 - Death of retired cotton
merchant Richard R Goodair
of Pownall Hall, 11 January

1896 - Henry Boddington,
magistrate, Mrs Goodier

1902 - Joseph Dickenson Lee

1910 - Ernest Theodore
Hilterman

1911 - William and Harriet
Brown

1920 - Sir Frank and Lady
Forbes Adam

1939 - Wilmslow College,
Alan P Clarke, headmaster

As well as being chairman of his own business, Boddington was one of the original directors of the Manchester Ship Canal Company and a substantial financial supporter. He was also chairman of both the Manchester Corn Exchange Building Company and British Maritime Company. He was much involved in the community, being a magistrate, a councillor for the Cheetham Ward of Manchester, a generous supporter of the arts, educational and library charities and a major backer of the 1887 Jubilee exhibition. The distinctive Mynshull House on Cateaton Street, Manchester, was built through the Mynshull Charity of which he was a trustee.

'Seven Ages of Man' by JD Watson

Unfortunately, by 1891 the Boddington family's finances were in decline following a failed business venture and over-generous gifts to friends. Henry resigned from his business interests and public duties and spent most of his remaining years at Estables, France, and at family lodgings in Guernsey. They returned to Britain as German forces advanced into France, to live at Gorsey Gate.

After Henry Boddington's death at Pownall Hall in 1925 aged 76, his ashes were scattered around the roots of the Ship Canal tree, as he had requested in his will. He was described in one obituary as 'a kindly, courteous gentleman'. A fellow magistrate said that he 'exercised great care and discretion' in his duties, and 'showed especial sympathy with the juvenile offenders'.

During Boddington's absence abroad, Richard Goodair, a retired Liverpool and Manchester cotton merchant and magistrate, lived at Pownall Hall for nearly two years until his death in 1894. By 1920 it was the home of Sir Frank and Lady Forbes Adam.

The hall was put up for sale in 1928 and there was speculation that it could be dismantled and shipped to New England, America, just as Agecroft Hall in Salford had been taken down in 1925 and rebuilt in Virginia. Interest in Pownall Hall was being shown by descendants of the families who had previously lived there.

The Carrs area of the estate, which Henry Boddington had generously given to Wilmslow, was officially handed over by his widow in 1930.

Pownall Hall and the dower house were unoccupied for some years up to 1933, and then most of the estate was sold off for housing, the remaining eight acres being bought by the Wilmslow College, which later became the Pownall Hall School. There had been proposals at that time to convert the hall into a hotel and sports club with a cricket ground and swimming pool.

Above: Carved inscription to the first owner of the hall, Richard de Pounale

Below: An earlier school advertisement

VIEW OF HOUSE.

POWNALL HALL,
WILMSLOW, CHESHIRE.

FOR BOYS FROM 6–14 YEARS (DAY AND BOARDING).

Principal:—ALAN P. CLARKE.

FOUNDED in 1895, the School removed to its present situation in 1934. It stands in 8½ acres of ground on a sandy subsoil.

All the teaching is planned by the Principal, who is assisted by a qualified staff. The chief aim is to develop initiative, personality, and responsibility.

Great stress is laid upon the necessity for games and hobbies. There is an up-to-date library which boys are encouraged to use to the fullest extent.

Mrs. Clarke, who holds a First Class Domestic Science Diploma, is assisted by two competent Matrons.

Fees:—Boarders 60 guineas a term. Day Boys, 25 guineas a term.

Prospectus on application.

Lindow

Above and Left: The heathland of Lindow is a 'Site of Special Scientific Interest'. There are few like it in Cheshire, and it used to stretch down to the Carrs by the river Bollin. It is the habitat for rare plants, insects and mammals. Black Lake was the venue for special events and where children sailed model boats. The site was given to the people of Wilmslow in 1897.

Below: Lindow Moss where commercial peat-cutters in August 1984 found the preserved body of man dating back to between 2 BC and 119 AD. The man was in his mid twenties and had died violently, perhaps in a ritualistic ceremony. The body was discovered when a workman removed what he thought was a piece of wood on the peat-shredding machine, but after the peat fell away, a human foot was revealed. The rest of the body was later unearthed by the County archaeologist and it became known as 'Lindow Man'. It is thought to be the best preserved bog body found in the UK. 'Pete Marsh' as he is nicknamed, is on display at the British Museum.

The previous year, workers found 'Lindow Woman' - a decomposing section of a human head with one eye and some hair still remaining, thought to date from 210 AD. The bog once covered over 1,500 acres and was considered a dangerous area after people either drowned there or had to be rescued.

Below: The flora and fauna on Lindow Moss, also known 'Saltersley Common' are threatened by the continued peat extraction. Plans have been submitted for housing on part of the site which is also in danger from a dropping water table.

STYAL

Above: Samuel Greg, founder of Styal cotton spinning mill. His son, Samuel, wrote that the best way to attract and retain a loyal and reliable work-force was: 'Fair wages, comfortable houses, gardens for their vegetables and flowers; schools and other means of improvement for their children; sundry little accommodations and conveniences in the mill, and interest in their general welfare'.

Quarry Bank Mill

The mill was founded by Samuel Greg, the son of a Belfast shipowner, in 1784. He chose this site because there was a 14ft fall in the Bollin here to turn the mill's two water wheels. He brought in business partner and engineer Peter Ewart, extended the premises and constructed a tunnel and wheel-race to increase efficiency. After Samuel Greg's death in 1834, power looms were introduced and the mill extended further in 1855.

Because of the initial shortage of labour in the small agricultural village of Styal, workers had to be found elsewhere. By 1790 the workforce comprised 183 adult workers obtained throughout the country from overseers of the poor, and 80 young apprentices from workhouses. Contracts were also made with the parents of older children for their services. Those in the south of England were brought to Styal by barge. No children under nine were employed and the workhouse apprentices were housed, fed and clothed by the company but received no wages. Other apprentices were paid between 9d and 1s 6d a week but had to pay for their own clothing. They worked 13-hour days except when the river Bollin was too low for production in the summer, and then the time was made up during the winter.

The working day in the 1830s began at 5.30am. There was a 10 minute break at 8.30am for breakfast, and 30 minutes for lunch at 1pm. Tea was taken at the machines at 5.50pm and work finished at 8pm - unless overtime was required. A succession of Factory Acts from 1833 until 1901 slowly improved the hours and working conditions. 9-11 year olds were allowed to work up to 9 hours daily, and 13 to18-year olds could work up to 12 hours in 1833. Shorter hours introduced in 1847 caused initial confusion among the workers who had been used to little else than bed and work. As a result of working a reduced week of just over fifty-five hours there was increased interest in sports such as football and cricket.

By 1875 children between 10 and 14 were to work only half a day, and women and older children for no more than 10 hours daily. Minimum working age was raised to 12 in 1901.

Working conditions were unpleasant - the air had to be kept hot and humid for the threads. There were many health risks at the mill. Workers suffered from lung disease by inhaling the cotton lint which stuck to clothing and hair. They had hearing problems from the long hours with the thundering machinery. Eyes were inflamed from the tallow lamps, cancer of the groin from the oil on the spindles and cancer of the mouth from 'kissing the shuttle', were other dangers. Also, bending at the machines caused deformities.

Styal provided the setting for a stable work-force, who remained with the company for many generations

Hannah, wife of Samuel Greg, did much for the welfare and education of the mill-workers. She believed everyone should aspire to better themselves, within their role in society. Hannah gave out the medicines prescribed by the doctor, and organised her own children to tutor the apprentices in reading and writing. She was devoutly religious and preached at the chapel, and probably founded the various clubs which supported the health needs of the workers.

The workers at first lived in enlarged houses and converted farm buildings but later Greg built homes for them. By the standards of the time they were better than the equivalent dwellings in the the towns. Styal's homes each had a privy and garden. They were separated by courts and alleys, rather than the 'back-to-back' as seen elsewhere.

Rents were deducted from the wages, with an average of eight people living in each cottage around 1850. There would have been little furniture in them. The cellars which originally may have been intended as loomshops were rented out separately to widows.

The village shop, run on a co-operative basis, opened in the 1820s, selling basic foods, clothing and household goods. It operated on a 'truck system' where the cost of the goods was automatically deducted from wages. At many mills, the owners abused the system and profited from it but the Gregs seem to have administered it fairly.

The Gregs provided a school, with the younger ones being taught in the daytime and the elder children in the evening. The 'half time' system which began in 1884 restricted children under 13 to six and a half hours' work a day and with up to five hours' schooling. Apprentices went one night a week. The girls were taught how to make their own clothes and shirts for the boys, and the boys had gardening lessons.

The men attended lectures from 1830 at the Mutual Improvement Society. Some of these were given by the Greg family. The mill family also established medical facilities, including a compulsory Sick Club, in which money was deducted from wages to pay for the treatment of illnesses and funeral expenses. There was a Female Society to deal with childbirth problems.

The apprentices were looked after by a doctor who visited the mill each week. He monitored new apprentices for a month to check if they were strong enough to work. Because of the rural situation and housing conditions, the people of Styal were healthy compared to those in the overcrowded grimy towns.

Discipline at the mill was maintained by a system of fines which were deducted from wages, rather than physical punishment. There was a five shilling fine for stealing an apple, and a quarter of a penny for breaking a window. However, a runaway girl was punished in 1836 by being locked in a room and given no lunch.

Several of the apprentices went on to hold important roles at the mill, such as mechanics and overlookers, one became book-keeper, another a school mistress, and two were promoted to manager.

Below: While the apprentices toiled long hours in the mill, the Greg children and their pets had time to play in the gardens and ride on a specially-constructed railway

Bottom: Mill-workers' homes, Oak Cottages. A visitor in 1836 wrote that the houses were 'commodious, clean, whitewashed and in every respect superior to the habitations for a similar class of labourers in the town ..'.

Two apprentice boys escaped from the mill in 1806 but were caught and brought before a Middlesex magistrate. One of them, Thomas, had some time before, lost a finger in a mill accident, and while he was recovering he thought about home. He said he had no complaint about life at Styal but had absconded because he wanted to see his mother .

Apprentice House

The Gregs took on many apprentices because they were inexpensive, easy to train and physically able to cope with the demanding work. In return, the Gregs were obliged to feed, clothe and house them. Up to a hundred apprentices lived at the house, built in 1790, under the supervision of a superintendent and his wife. They slept in long rooms, two to a bed, with the boys separated from the girls.

William Rathbone Greg gave evidence to a Parliamentary Committee in 1833 that most of the apprentices came from the Liverpool Poorhouse, the majority being female. Greg said that most of the apprentices married amongst themselves and remained at the mill. Over the years they had taken on about 550 apprentices.

In 1841 it was home for 32 apprentices between the age of 15 and 9 under the supervision of George Henshall, a grocer. In later years after the apprentice system was abandoned, it was used by other mill workers including James Kinsey, the mill manager, in 1871. Richard Mallinson, a retired jailer from Knutsford Prison, was the head of the household in 1881. He had been an instructor of wool-sorting at the prison.

Left : Beatrice (Bessy) Mary Greg, great grand-daughter of Samuel Greg, lived at the Apprentice House until her death in 1938. She was a spinster and when she was invalided she travelled around in a basket carriage pulled by her faithful donkey 'Jenny'. She usually had her dog

Above and inset: Beatrice Greg

in her lap as she chatted to the locals while travelling around the neighbourhood. Bessy was also a generous benefactor to anyone in need. She died within a month of her housekeeper and companion, Miss Minnie Longworth.

Samuel H Henshall, the mill manager, was living at the house in 1911, and remained there until the working mill's closure. In 1971 it was also the home of John Brierley and family, the National Trust's manager of Styal. The Apprentice House is now used for tours led by costumed guides.

The mill and the Styal estate were given to the National Trust in 1939. Production of cotton cloth stopped in 1956 and the mill closed three years later. The mill, village, woods and river became Styal Country Park in 1973. Quarry Bank Mill opened as a museum in 1976.

The gardens which opened in 2008 at Quarry Bank beside the river Bollin

The apprentice children attended Wilmslow Church twice on Sundays as required by law. The girls wore straw bonnets and grey dresses, and the boys had fustian coats and corduroy breeches.

Samuel Greg built Norcliffe Chapel (below) for the villagers in 1823. It was originally a Baptist Chapel but later became Unitarian. Robert Hyde Greg added a porch and other extensions.

A Methodist Society was formed in the village, and met in cottages and farmhouses before moving into their own chapel in 1837.

Quarry Bank House

Built in 1787 and extended in 1802 with stables and outbuildings, it was the home of Samuel Greg and family. A 19th century visitor wrote 'The house over which this excellent woman (Mrs Greg) presided offered an ideal picture of domestic felicity ...the absence of display, and even knick-knacks, the plain blue walls, the comfortable furniture, the well-filled book-cases, the portrait of George Washington over the mantelpiece'.

After Samuel's death in 1834, it was lived in by his grandson Edward Hyde Greg. Edward's brother, Robert Alexander Greg, was the next occupant until 1906. Noel Lee, a director of Tootal Broadhurst and Lee, Oxford Street Manchester followed at Quarry Bank. He was also Brigadier-General and Commander of the Manchester Infantry Brigade of the East Lancashire Territorial Division. He died from wounds fighting in the Dardanelles in 1915 during the Gallipoli Campaign in Turkey. After WW1 it was leased by Col. EW Greg to LL Samuels. In the 1950s the house was occupied by Mr T Hilldrup, and by Eric Lowcock in the 1970s. The house is now owned by the National Trust who have plans to re-open it to the public.

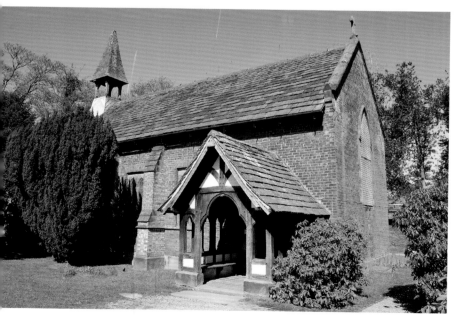

Above: Sandstone quarry by the Bollin used for building the mill
Below: The walk between the Carrs and Styal mill

Norcliffe Hall

The hall was completed in 1831 by Lichfield architect Thomas Johnson for Robert Hyde Greg at a cost of around £2000. Greg moved there from rented accommodation in Manchester in order to be close to his mill at Quarry Bank. A tower and billiard room were added in 1860.

Greg was interested in horticulture and the gardens were noted for the conifers and rhododendrons. He also built a stone circle and a folly ruin in the landscaped grounds. The family were also responsible for the planting of Californian redwood trees in the woods. There used to be a red-stone plaque which stated that the trees, now around 350 feet high, were three feet tall when planted in 1838. In an 1876 advertisement, the public wanting to visit the gardens had to apply in writing or, if a friend or acquaintance, leave their card or name at the lodge. Later, because of vandalism, the grounds were closed to the public.

Greg and his wife and family travelled around Europe and North Africa and made sketches and watercolours of the sights they had seen. He was the second of Samuel Greg's thirteen children,

and became the most able of the four brothers who ran the Greg mills. He was regarded by the villagers as being rather reserved but was an energetic and shrewd businessman who managed to keep Styal Mill profitable and avoid some of the pitfalls experienced in the uncertain textile industry by his brothers and his son. He was generous in financial support for others in the family and willing to offer advice. But the strain of business along with his other public duties led him to suffer with severe headaches and anxiety, and his journeys abroad were partly to help him recover from the stress of his busy life.

He had been one of the strongest campaigners in support of repealing the Corn Laws, and published many pamphlets on the subject. Until the repeal of the law in 1846, cheaper foreign imports had been barred which forced up the price of bread in the UK. But Greg also argued that mill-owners should not be restricted in the length of the working day, in order to keep mills profitable and people in employment.

He was a reluctant MP in Manchester for the (Parliamentary) Reform Party in 1839, involved with the Manchester Mechanics Institute, and a member of the Manchester Geological Society. In his later years, he retired from business life and concentrated on the cultivation of the Norcliffe estate and also Coles Park in Hertfordshire which he had inherited from his elder brother, until he died in 1875 aged 79. It is said that deer roamed freely around the Norcliffe grounds and that one barged into him, causing permanent damage to his health.

In the 1881 Census, three of the children of CP Scott, editor of the 'Manchester Guardian' newspaper, were being looked after by the Hall staff. They were the nephews and niece of Miss Isabella Scott who lived there. The children were Lawrence, who became an active supporter at the Manchester University Settlement at Ancoats Hall, died from TB age 31; John who went on to be manager of the Guardian and founder of the Scott Trust newspaper group, and Madeline who married journalist and author CE Montague. Their son Eleyn, also a journalist, featured in the famous 'Chariots of Fire' film. Another of CP Scott's children, Edward, succeeded his father as Editor of the newspaper but was tragically drowned in a sailing accident on Lake Windermere within three years of taking up the role.

Theodore Crewdson, a commission agent and JP, lived there at the hall between around 1896 and 1904.

Robert Hyde Greg, son of Samuel who introduced weaving to Styal mill which continued in commercial operation until 1959.

Robert confirmed in a memorandum that his father had changed the local name where the mill was located from 'Ferney Brow' to 'Quarry Bank'. This was over fears that the use of 'Ferney', which had been the name of the Swiss home of writer Voltaire who had stirred up the French Revolution, could potentially cause trouble amongst the workers in England.

Later, Edward Hyde (1827-1910), second son of Robert lived at Norcliffe. As a senior partner in the family business, he was prominent in the cotton trade, a regular attender at the Manchester Royal Exchange and also a director of the Royal Assurance Company. He was Deputy Lieutenant for Cheshire, a JP, magistrate and a member of Wilmslow and Cheshire County Council. He served as an officer in the Cheshire Rifle Volunteers, the Cheshire Yeomanry and the 4th Royal Lancashire Militia. Edward was keen on sport, shooting and fishing and had travelled around the world.

In 1895 he had a narrow escape while out in his horse and carriage (dogcart) in Gatley. As he drove through the village, the horse suddenly shied and veered onto the footpath and he was thrown out of the cab and into the road and knocked unconscious. He regained consciousness and was taken to a nearby cottage to recover. Although he had cuts to his face and injuries to his wrist, shoulder and thigh, he was well enough to be brought home. Later his doctor thought that Greg's hat which remained on his head throughout the accident, had probably saved him from more serious injury. He died five years later aged 82.

Lily became head-housemaid at Norcliffe in 1907. In reminiscences to her daughter VL Clift she described the working conditions and the attitude of the Gregs towards the servants. Lily was paid £22 a year and had to pay for her own uniform. Her employees seemed pleasant and kind, but it was understood that she never queried anything they asked her to do because that would have meant instant dismissal. Her working day began at 6.30am and ended once all the beds had hot water bottles and the Greg family had retired. She had one free afternoon a fortnight in which she used to cycle with another maid to Stockport or Manchester. However, when the family went away on holiday in August, once the household chores were completed, Lily was free to cycle further afield, reaching as far as Delamere Forest.

Colonel Ernest William (1862-1934), son of Edward, was listed at Norcliffe in 1911. He had served in local government for Lancashire and Cheshire County Councils, and on Bucklow District Council. In military service, he was a leading figure in the Territorial Army as commander of various regiments and battalions in Cheshire and Wales. He was twice mentioned in dispatches during World War I when he was in his fifties. Tragically, two of his sons were killed during the conflict. In 1925 he was made honorary Colonel of the 7th Battalion Cheshire Regiment.

Edward Hyde Greg

Colonel Ernest Greg

He gave much attention to the welfare of his employees at Eagley mills, Bolton as well as enjoying travelling around the world, which made him a fitting president of Manchester Geographical Society, holding some of the society's meetings at Norcliffe. He was also a fellow of the Royal Geographical Society. He was said to be an entertaining and considerate host, and well-read with a vast range of knowledge.

Colonel Greg before his death had wanted to give Quarry Bank Mill, the village and the estate to the National Trust and it was finally handed over in 1939 by Alec Greg, who had spent his childhood at Norcliffe Hall and was the great-great-grandson of the founder of the mill, Samuel Greg.

Norcliffe was sold in March 1948 to Captain Harold Garfit Watts. His grandfather, Dr John Watts, originated the idea of a free lending library in Manchester in 1850. With the help of Mayor, Sir John Potter, he was able to establish the first library of its kind following a Parliamentary Act two years later. It meant the less well-off had access to periodicals, newspapers and books to read or to borrow from well-lit and warm buildings. By 1974 Norcliffe was owned by Mrs J Higham but in 1988 it was controversially made into a nursing home, and then in about 2009 the grade II listed building was converted into eight private apartments.

Norcliffe Hall owners & occupiers

1831 - Robert H Greg, cotton manufacturer

1871 - Samuel Greg, magistrate and landowner

1878 - Widow of RH Greg

1896 - Theodore Crewdson

1901 - Theodore Crewdson

1911 - Col Ernest W Greg

1934 - Col Ernest W Greg

1939 - HG Watts

1988 - Hall became nursing home - now private apartments

Above top: The Bollin at Giant's Castle

Above: Butterbur, also known as 'Bog rhubarb' and 'Pestilence Wort' by the Bollin near Styal

Right: The exit of the three quarters of a mile long tunnel from Styal mill into the Bollin. The contractor used only picks and shovels and could not sign his own name. Construction began in 1817 and took two years. The work overseen by Samuel Greg involved the mill apprentices on overtime, and cost £2005 13s in labour charges. The tunnel enabled the water to get away from the mill more quickly, which led to a new larger mill wheel and increased production.

RINGWAY

The Romper

The 1894 Chapel building closed in 1970

Previous page: Manchester Airport runway which passes over the river Bollin

Below: Concorde on display before the building of the new hangar

Ringway

The area once known as 'Ringey' used to be an isolated hamlet with a few farms, All Saints church and the Romper inn. There has been a chapel here since the 16th century and the pub began as 'The Red Lion', but locals re-named the young lion on the inn sign as 'the romping kitlin' which evolved into the present name.

In 1929 Ringway became the site of the country's first municipal airport, operating on a temporary licence for a few months until Barton airport was prepared. It was later decided that Ringway had more capacity for expansion and land was purchased for £80,000. It officially opened in 1938 but closed the following year with the outbreak of WW2. Ringway's grass landing strip was not suitable for military aircraft and it became a centre for aircraft manufacture and training parachutists. Converted Whitley bombers were used for the training jumps, but they also used a simulated exit from a hole in the hangar. The parachutists found it a tight fit to get through with all their kit and many painfully caught their chins on the edge, an experience which was known as 'the Whitley kiss'.

Ringway was renamed 'Manchester International Airport' in 1975, and one of the greatest events in its history was the first arrival of Concorde in May 1980. Roads around the airport were gridlocked as thousands came to get their first glance of this famous aircraft. At Styal, much to the annoyance of a farmer, some motorists parked on a newly-ploughed and seeded field.

Following the decommissioning of the twenty Concordes in 2003, Manchester Airport now has one of them on permanent display. Concorde G-BOAC is housed in a £1million hanger and visitor centre at the Aviation Viewing Park. She had flown for twenty-seven years and was the fastest commercial airliner of all time after flying at 1,488mph. It is interesting to note that her 204ft length is longer than the Wright brothers' first flight.

The legal and security costs against the campaign exceeded £3 million. During the five month confrontation, one of the security guards resigned his job and joined the protesters.

The building of a second runway, opened in 2001, had a significant impact on the Bollin Valley. Ancient woodlands and wild life habitats were lost despite the campaign of opposition from 'eco warriors' such as 'Swampy'. The Airport compensated for the loss of the land by creating new woodlands, grasslands and ponds around the runway. About 37,000 amphibians were collected and relocated to the ponds, and three barns were constructed to allow bats to roost.

At the development site, archaeologists found the remains of a pre-historic settlement close to the river Bollin at Oversley Farm. Pottery was discovered from this ancient farmstead, which was later occupied by the Romans. Evidence of farm buildings dating from Medieval times was also unearthed.

Runway extension workings by the Bollin

Airport activity as seen from the Viewing Park, with Kinder Scout, Derbyshire, in the background

The tunnel which takes the airport's second runway over the river Bollin is an impressive structure - 270m long, 18m high and 24m wide

Although the sound of the aircraft dominates this part of the Bollin Valley and the landscape has been dramatically changed, serious effort has been made to conserve the wildlife of the area. There are bat roosting chambers on the roof of the tunnel and additional nesting sites for bats and birds at each end. The river water is aerated by a series of small waterfalls which encourage the passage of fish, such as brown trout, to swim through the tunnel. Tree trunks along the wall protect mammals as they pass through

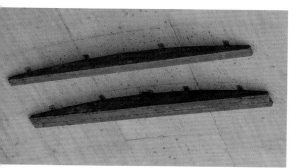

119

The first Manchester Airport runway was extended by 800ft in 1981. The river Bollin had to be diverted, and a weir and stilling pond constructed to slow the flow of the water. Parts of Double Wood were covered by an 82ft high by 360ft long embankment. Rare species of plants were removed and planted elsewhere. During the building of the second runway, ancient trees in Arthur's wood were felled or pollarded. A listed barn in Mobberley on the site of the proposed second runway was taken down and rebuilt six miles away in Nether Alderley.

Here are scenes of the 'lost Bollin' - areas changed by the construction of Manchester Airport's runway extensions, including (left) the big cliff by the Bollin, next to Oversley Ford clay pit.

Lionel Willshaw

Lionel Willshaw

Lionel Willshaw

Opposite page: Watch Hill earthworks, Bowdon

AROUND ASHLEY

In the memorial stone:

IN MEMORY OF
THOMAS ALFRED COWARD
1867-1933
COTTRILL CLOUGH AND MARBURY REED BED
WERE PURCHASED BY PUBLIC SUBSCRIPTION
TO REMAIN FOR EVER UNDISTURBED
AS A MEMORIAL TO HIS GREAT SERVICES
TO NATURAL SCIENCE

The steep-sided clough has a stream which runs into the Bollin

Cotterill Clough

The site has long been a haven of natural and wild-life, and has attracted naturalists since the late 1700s. It was for many years privately owned and guarded by gamekeepers. Anyone thinking about trespassing would have been warned by wooden signs reading 'Spring Guns and Man Traps'. Some have thought that Spring comes to the Bollin Valley earlier than other places with a carpeting of greenery followed by a wide range of wild flowers. The eminent botanist Leo Grindon wrote of the valley in 1858 that the blooming primroses had no equal in this part of the country.

In the early 1930s the surrounding woods began to be felled. There was also concern that the building of the outdoor pool at Castle Mill would disturb the beauty and peace of the area. It was decided to purchase Cotterill Clough, by public subscription, as a nature reserve in memory of Thomas Coward, the Bowdon naturalist.

Enough money was raised to also purchase Marbury Reedbed. The clough was officially opened in 1934 and is a 14-acre site designated as of special scientific interest. It came under threat during the building of the second runway at Manchester Airport when there were proposals to cut down trees on the perimeter.

Thomas Coward

Born in Bowdon in 1867, he inherited his father's love of natural history. He was honorary curator at Manchester Museum and Manchester University where he was also acting keeper during WW1. He was a popular lecturer on Cheshire customs and history at both university and county secondary schools. Coward taught at Heyrod St Ancoats, Manchester and founded the Lads' Club there. He was not only a keen walker, climber and astronomer but also wrote books and newspaper articles about the Cheshire countryside; he travelled widely and was an expert on the land and sea birds of the Hebrides. He died in January 1933 and there is a blue plaque outside his former home, 10 Grange Road, Bowdon.

● The clough is a restricted site, and anyone wanting to visit should apply to the Cheshire Wildlife Trust.

Pool cafe

Jackson's brickworks

Castle Mill Swimming Pool

The 160ft long by 60ft wide pool opened in the summer of 1933, using water filtered from the Bollin. It was built by Herbert Lawrence and his brother using bricks to line the pool made at the nearby Jackson's Brickworks - close to the present site of Manchester Airport's second runway. They were assisted by unemployed builders and farm hands. Herbert Lawrence acquired adjoining land later that year, and construction work continued through the following winter with the building of a 75ft long children's pool, thatched cafe, tennis court and a bridge over the Bollin. The site was landscaped with flower beds, shrubs and trees, and on sunny days attracted big crowds. New features for 1934 included an extended car-park, camp site, floodlighting, and deepening the diving end of the pool. All-age free swimming tuition was introduced at the August Bank Holiday.

The remote location at Ashley meant that visitors needed transport to get there. Many cars parked on Mill Lane next to the site causing problems for farmers, especially at hay-making times trying to get through with their tractors and waggons. A farmer who lives opposite the old pool remembered hordes of people flocking to the area and bathing in the Bollin. Unfortunately there were many broken glass bottles in the river in those days, and he and his wife treated lots of people with cut feet. People also recall having to pull off leeches after going in the river. One local remembers, as a lad, going to the pool late in the day and swimming along the bottom where they found money. On one occasion he found a ring with his own initials on it.

One visitor remembered when there were weeds and frogs in the pool during a period when it was not well maintained. He was intrigued by the rustic screen

Above: Castle mill pool c1935. Note the rustic fence between the pool and the paddling pool which was later removed
Below: map of the site c1960

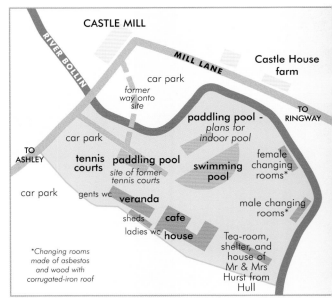

CASTLE MILL

RIVER BOLLIN

MILL LANE

Castle House farm

car park

former way onto site

TO ASHLEY

car park

car park

tennis courts

paddling pool
site of former tennis courts

gents wc

veranda

sheds

ladies wc

cafe

house

paddling pool -
plans for indoor pool

TO RINGWAY

swimming pool

female changing rooms*

male changing rooms*

Tea-room, shelter, and house of Mr & Mrs Hurst from Hull

*Changing rooms made of asbestos and wood with corrugated-iron roof

Rustic bridge from car park

The cafe

covered in roses which separated the two pools. The opening of the Lido indoor swimming pool in Sale with its entertainment and the Miss Sale Lido competition, drew him away from Castle Mill.

The 1934 handbook for the Castle Mill site makes amusing reading to the present day reader, '...here at last is the place the jaded worker sighs for in the summer's heat. Here is the place for a splash, a swim, or a frolic in cool clean water...'. As regards young people they 'have to be watched carefully in case they overtax their strength, and it needs an experienced eye, and a word at the correct moment, to guard against over-exertion'.

The site was open from 7am to 10pm with the grounds floodlit so that 'those who had enjoyed the zest of the day can relax and enjoy an entirely different aspect of the grounds...' The good catering was highlighted - locally-grown salads, refrigerated ice cream made with real cream ...'What a place is this Cheshire!' Miniten, a smaller version of tennis was another attraction. In terms of safety the guide stated 'The Pool is always under the surveillance of capable swimmers, and inflated belts in abundance are always in easy reach.'

Winter 1963-64: top River Bollin, below: outdoor pool

Lionel Willshaw

However in August 1935 a young man from West Bromwich became the first person to die at the pool. He and his younger cousin were the only ones in the water, but following a dive and resurfacing, he was next seen below the water with bubbles rising to the surface. The alarm was raised but the two attendants had to change into their bathing costumes before they rescued him. They tried artificial respiration but to no avail.

At the inquest in Altrincham, Mr Lawrence the owner, said that since the opening 50,000 people had safely used the pool. There were always five people on call to rescue people. It is surprising that no-one spotted sooner the deceased who was wearing a red swimming costume and, with only one other in the water, had got into difficulty. The doctor who conducted the postmortem concluded that death had been caused by the sudden plunge into bitterly cold water.

After Walter and Mabel Haddon took over ownership in 1940, there was a further drowning tragedy five years later. Two boys aged nine and eleven from Timperley had gone to the pool with their parents, but unnoticed, they seemed to have strayed into the deep end and got into difficulties. It was later noted that there were no signs indicating the depth of water at the time, because people repeatedly removed the boards.

Mr Haddon said at the inquest that he had been on duty and tried to keep his eye on all the bathers, but admitted it was not possible to see the bottom of the pool because it had been discoloured by rain water. When the boys' parents raised the alarm, another bather dived in but was hampered by the dark conditions below the surface. Searchers eventually located the boys by touch. The ambulance sent to the incident from Altrincham did not have oxygen and another appliance had to be sent for with the correct equipment.

When the Coroner later visited the pool, he described the water as being in a filthy state and looking more like a stagnant pool. He questioned the standards of safety at the pool and wondered why it had never been officially inspected. Mr Haddon had been seen chalking the depth of the pool on a board an hour after the tragedy. No further action was taken against the management, and a verdict of misadventure returned. The local authority later confirmed they had no legal powers to inspect private pools.

Lionel Willshaw

Above: A more peaceful day at the pool. Below: The site of the pool (on left) before its construction in 1933.

Hale Civic Society

Changing room tokens

A planning application was submitted to Bucklow Council to extend the tea room in March 1951, but it was refused because the original building had never received planning permission. Water for the pools was later supplied by Manchester Corporation, and had to undergo local authority inspections.

Stuart Willshaw was the next owner of the pool in the summer of 1951 in partnership with Reginald Bowran, and various improvements were made. During the winter Willshaw did the maintenance work on the site but was also employed at the Oversleyford brick works, now covered by the second runway at Manchester Airport. Later he became the sole proprietor of the pool.

Lionel Willshaw

Lionel Willshaw

Lionel Willshaw

Top: View from the top of an oak tree

Above: Owner Stuart Willshaw (left) with life-saver George Roberts from Chorlton

Right top: Gardens in bloom

Right below: Traffic congestion in Mill Lane

Visitors paid at the kiosk (towards the top of photograph) to gain entry. Some came by the single-decker bus which stopped at Castle Mill. Hawaiian dancing girls were one of the advertised evening attractions, but the event was often rained off. The cafe offered drinks, sandwiches and salads but not full meals. When it rained, visitors sheltered under the verandas, and there would be a loud cheer on the site when the sun came out. The actor, Robert Morley, is said to have been a regular visitor to the tearoom in the 1960s.

Right: The top field for additional parking which regularly had to be cleared of nettles

Lionel Willshaw

Peace returns to Castle Mill

As the days get shorter and winter approaches, a little spot in the Cheshire countryside becomes peaceful again. Until last week, and for the past five months, it has been the retreat for thousands of get-away-from-it-all people. The scene — Castle Mill, Ashley, and its open air swimming pools and gardens — has been cared for by Mr Stuart Willshaw and his wife Dorothy for the past 20 years. Castle Mill closed its doors last weekend for the season after a record attendance figure and for Mr and Mrs Willshaw now starts the long winter battle to prepare for next year's invasion.

Lionel Willshaw

133

OPEN DAILY from 10 a.m. to 10 p.m

Castle Mill Swimming Pool
Ashley, Nr. Altrincham

EXCELLENT TEA GARDENS

Your Resident Host
Mr. JOHN SYKES

Telephone :
928-1435

Cheshire County Council considered purchasing the site when the pool and five and a half acres of land were put up for sale in 1969 for £25,000. Frank Mitchell, owner of the Bredbury Hall nightclub, bought the site and placed it under the management of John Sykes, who fitted a new filtration system to make the water clearer. He also organised evening events.

A Guardian article and photograph of Castle Mill in August 1973 reported that during the hot weather thousands had flocked to the pool as they had done for years. However, Mitchell obtained planning permission to close the pool in 1974 and replace the existing bungalow on the site with a new house. The pool closed in about 1978 and a large house now stands on the site. The interior of the house was used during the filming of the TV drama 'Life on Mars'. The old pool is still remembered with great affection by thousands of people who flocked there on sunny days.

Above: John Sykes - Castle Mill Pool's last manager
Above right: The house built by Frank Mitchell
Opposite page: Sunbank Wood

Left: Sunbank wood
Inset: Nuthatch
Below left: WW2 gun mounting
in Sunbank wood to defend
the bridge at Castle Mill
Below right: The Bollin
at Castle Mill
Bottom: Castle Mill c1910

Castle Mill

The plaque on the existing building suggests it dates back to 1808 but it has been the site of a corn mill for many centuries. In one of the earliest references to the mill, John de Muredon, bailiff of Dunham Massey, lists Castle Mill as costing £4 11s 10d in September 1363. In 1417 repairs to the mill came to 37s 8d and a new mill wheel cost 16s. By 1540 William Chauntrell earned 40s annual rent from the mill. The 'castle' referred to may have been a 12th-century fortification next to Castle Hill farm, south-east of the mill.

John Brereton lived at the mill in about 1672 and was licensed to hold dissenting religious meetings there because it was within five miles of his previous churches at Ringway and Wilmslow where he was the minister. This was permitted under the new promise of religious toleration given by Charles II.

Above: The platform by the door on the left, was at tailboard height for loading onto carts c1905. One former local remembers a bus time-table attached to the mill wall here, by a bus stop.

Castle Mill c1910, from a painting by H Meadows

Mrs Pownall

When the mill came to be auctioned in 1817 it had a 'constant and regular supply of water, a powerful waterwheel, two pairs of mill-stones for grinding wheat, one pair of stones for grinding oatmeal, and one pair of shelling mill-stones'.

There had been a member of the Jackson family at the mill for much of the nineteenth century, starting with Thomas in about 1840. Richard Jackson, who retired in 1906, had been the miller there for over forty years. He was also a farmer and had lived at Castle Mill farm and was one of the best-known cattle breeders in Cheshire. He died in 1908 at his home on Westgate, Hale. Richard's nephew of the same name started at the mill in 1906 and then carried on the business after his uncle's death. Born at Dairyhouse Farm Broadheath, he became well known in the district as a miller and farmer, and died in 1944 aged 81.

Above: Plaque from the old mill on the house at the site, with the date of its rebuilding

Below: Assheton grave at Bowdon Church

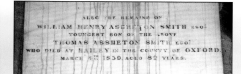

The mill was not an easy place to access for horse and carts with steep inclines in either direction, as well as the rounded cobbles on Mill Lane which were difficult for both horse and driver. Severe storms in June 1872 caused havoc throughout the Bollin Valley. At Castle Mill the weir was destroyed, the mill was flooded and corn lost. At the nearby Castle Mill farm, the sow and her litter were washed away.

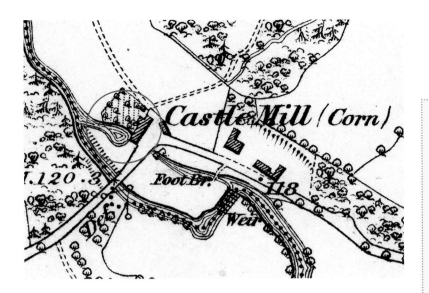

Millers

1778 - 1832 land tax assessments - owned by William Assheton Smith

1817 - Mill for sale following the bankcruptcy of John Croft. The mill had been occupied by Joseph Fenna.

1818 - James Davenport

Tithe map c1840 - owned by William Egerton, occupied by Thomas Jackson

1841 - Thomas Jackson, miller (In 1851 he was farming at Hasty Lane, Hale)

1851 - Sarah Massey, miller (In 1841 she and her husband were millers at the Moreton Mill, Astbury)

1855 - Massey & Son

1857 - Partnership dissolved between Thomas Jackson and James Jackson corn dealers, flour dealers and millers, of Castle Mill, 17th January. Business carried on by Thomas and by Richard, late of Ashley.

1861 - Thomas Jackson and brother Richard, corn miller and farmer employing 5 men and 1 boy

1871 - Richard Jackson

1891 - Richard Jackson - living at Castle House. Thomas Moult living at Castle Mill

1906 - Richard's nephew, of the same name, took over the business

1934 - Richard Jackson, miller

Remains of the mill weir c1920

It was reported that after the flood had subsided there remained a two feet-deep bed of sand.

The mill had been derelict since about 1934 as business declined, and was demolished in Spring 1954. A large water-wheel and rusting machinery were all that remained of the mill. The present house was built the following year, with the plaque on the front of the mill updated and installed over the garage. William Henry Assheton Smith, of Ashley Hall, was the builder of the mill, and taxed for Castle Mill between 1778 and 1832. There is a memorial to him in Bowdon Church. John Pierson was the under-tenant at Castle Mill in 1793.

Above & below: Ross Mill farm and barn

Ross Mill

It was known over the centuries as 'Rasse Mill' until about 1855. The mill is mentioned in documents in 1289 when it was part of the lands granted to Jurdon de Davenport. The farm of the same name is some way up the hill from the Bollin and it is not known where the mill was located. The mill was repaired at a cost of 7s 1d, and supplied with a new millstone for 16s in 1417.

Isaac Harrop, one of the biggest landowners in the district, held the property from the 1830s. Born in 1777, he became a solicitor in Altrincham, but later withdrew from the profession to concentrate on looking after his growing land acquisitions through inheritance and marriage. He was Mayor of Altrincham in 1835 and 1836, and in his later years was a magistrate and a keen supporter of civic and religious freedom. His father was the minister at Hale Chapel for 46 years.

Annie Elizabeth Harrop was a descendant of Isaac and she married Charles Henry Wolff, a cotton merchant and farmer. By 1891 they had moved to Ross Mill. Their son, Robert Harrop, was secretary of Hale Chapel and re-opened the working men's club in Hale Barns. Their eldest son, Arnold Harrop, was a great sporting all-rounder, playing for Cheshire at tennis, golf and rugby. For nine years he played centre forward in the North of England hockey team, and was a player with Manchester Rugby Club. Like his father, he loved cricket and was a notable wicket-keeper, but also won many trophies in miniature rifle shooting. Arnold was a founder member of Hale Golf Club, which was on the Wolff estate, helping to set out the greens. When he died aged 80, in 1948, he was still interested in sport and had recently been to Wimbledon and to watch Lancashire at Old Trafford.

Charles Henry Wolff

Owners and occupiers

1841 - William Warburton

1851 - William Warburton (Rass Mill) farmer

1871 - James Whalley, (Rass Mill) farmer of 93 acres (in 1861 a bricklayer at Long Lane, Hale)

1873 - OS map - 'Ross Mill'

1901 - Lewis J Whalley (son of James), farmer

1911 - Arnold Harrop Wolff, farmer

Hale Golf Club

The nine hole course, set in picturesque surroundings on the banks of the Bollin, was founded on land belonging to Ross Mill Farm in 1903. The original lease stipulated there was to be no play on Sundays, and that sheep and cattle could continue to graze there. This prompted a new rule - 'If a golf ball lay on or within six inches of manure, it could be 'dropped' or repositioned just behind without penalty'.

By the time of WW1 there was no livestock on the course but during the last World War, parts of the course were dug up to grow crops.

The 1919 club suggestion book highlighted hygiene problems for the members. There was a request that the club hairbrush should be washed again, following its clean two years previously!

Hale Chapel built 1723

Left & below: Known as the 'bomb ponds', they were created by a bomb during the Blitz in January 1941 when many bombs dropped on the area. It is not known whether the enemy pilots were just jettisoning the bombs or were trying to hit nearby Ringway airport.

Lancashire county Cricket Club Archives

The Flying Cricketer

Above: Peter Eckersley, captain of Lancashire County Cricket Club

Above right: Eckersley (middle)

Below:'Midway' home of Peter Eckersley, and the adjoining field where he landed his plane

'Midway' close to the centre of Ashley was the home of Peter Thorpe Eckersley, who captained Lancashire County Cricket Club in their Championship wins of 1930 and 1934. He was nicknamed 'the flying cricketer' because he often flew himself to matches. Eckersley used to land his plane in a field next to the house, after his chauffeur had waved a rag to test the wind direction. In 1935 he arranged for the whole team to be flown from Cardiff to Southampton on the 51-minute journey in two planes, which was the first time it had happened in county cricket.

He was one of the 'gentlemen cricketers' who were supposedly amateur, although it is thought he was paid 'expenses' by the club. Eckersley made his debut for Lancashire in 1923 making a 'duck', and took over the captaincy in 1926. He played for the MCC and his final match was for an England X1 in 1938.

Eckersley moved to 'Midway' with his family in 1933 and had a billiard room extension built. He had given up politics to play cricket but in 1935 he resigned to become the MP for Manchester Exchange. During WW2 he was a lieutenant in the Air Arm of the Royal Naval Volunteer Reserve, and died in a flying accident at Eastleigh, Hampshire in August 1940 at the age of 36. He could have claimed exemption from war service as an MP, and was one of five Lancashire cricketers who became Members of Parliament.

Ashley Hall

It is a site of great antiquity with the remains of a Roman ironworks found here. By the thirteenth century, at the time of King John, a hunting lodge was situated here. The present hall dates back to 1490 when it was a three-storey manor house. Mary Queen of Scots is said to have lodged here for the night on her way to imprisonment at Beeston Castle.

The estate belonged for several centuries to the Dutton family who later changed their name to Ashley. There is an old coat of arms of George Ashley of Ashley and his wife Cicely Sutton in the roof space, which is thought to date to sometime before 1580.

The hall was later the ancestral seat of the Breretons, the last at Ashley being Sir William Brereton, one of Oliver Cromwell's commanders. There is a tradition that Jane Brereton, whose effigy is at Bowdon Church, was murdered at Ashley Hall. The estate passed to the Assheton family with the marriage of Catherine to Ralph Assheton.

William and Jane Brereton tomb at Bowdon Church

Above top left: The 16th century Ashley family crest in the roofspace of the hall

In 1715 eleven Cheshire squires met at the hall, then the home of Thomas Assheton, Governor of Chester Castle, to discuss whether they should continue to support the new King - George I, or back Charles Stuart with whom they had strong sympathies. As news came through of Jacobite defeats and also details of cruel treatment given to the king's enemies, they decided to remain with the king which proved to be a wise decision and possibly saved their lives. It was Assheton's casting vote that ensured they stayed loyal to the king.

Afterwards, perhaps in thanks to Assheton and in celebration, the squires had full-length portraits painted of themselves and hung in the drawing room at Ashley Hall. The paintings, dated 1720, have the subjects dressed in the frock coats and slashed sleeves, court swords by their sides, with broad-toed shoes and buckles of the period. The paintings were removed by Lord Egerton in 1860, when he had them restored and later displayed on the upper landing at Tatton, where they can be seen today. Ashley Hall's 'elegant household furniture' was auctioned at Knutsford in December 1783.

Ashley Hall remained in the Assheton family until Lord Egerton purchased it from Thomas Assheton Smith in 1846. Thomas had not lived in the hall and was an outstanding all-round sportsman. Within cricket circles he was known as the 'British Nimrod' because of his impressive batting performances. He had been MP for Andover and Caernarvonshire, and High Sheriff of Wiltshire and was a well-known foxhunter. Lord Egerton made Ashley a dower house for Tatton Hall, and removed the third storey.

Farm buildings

John Hill came from Chester to live at the hall sometime after 1817. He was the Attorney-General for Cheshire and North Wales. Robert, his father, was a Cheshire magistrate and clergyman. Sir Rowland Hill, his grandfather, owned and developed the famous Hawkstone Park estate in Shropshire. In 1829 John Hill attended a meeting at the George Inn, Knutsford campaigning against further concessions to Roman Catholics.

He and his wife complained to Lord Stamford in 1834 about the behaviour of the organist at Bowdon Church. During the absence of the vicar, he had been playing waltzes, quadrilles and ballads during the services and had accompanied the singers in an 'extremely violent and noisy manner'.

By 1835 Hill was Assistant Barrister in Manchester. It was reported in 1828 that three men stole fruit and produce from the extensive gardens at Ashley. Produce from the Hall estate won Hill a number of competitions between 1835 and 1837. The 1838 tithe map shows that there was a lake to the south of the hall on the 11-acre grounds. Around 1841 he moved to Standish Hall, and he died aged 74 in 1849 while staying at Worleston Rookery, Nantwich.

His youngest son, Major Rowland Hill, commanded the 4th Irregular Cavalry Bengal Army. They wore distinctive coloured coats and were known as 'the yellow boys'. The irregular cavalries were less disciplined, and attracted men and British officers of free spirit. William Taylor who travelled with Hill in India, described him as '... a gentleman not unknown to fame or fortune, a tried soldier, untiring itinerant, inveterate sportsman, cherisher of a (large) beard ... and last but not least, a right merry companion.'

Taylor also described a turnout of Hill's cavalry in his journal: 'This evening Major Hill held a parade of his regiment, a pretty and

The cellar is quite small, although there is evidence of a blocked-off entrance. There was reputedly an underground passage by which the priest could escape to the fields, during times of religious persecution

148

exciting sight it was. The bright yellow dresses and red breeches, high boots and steel caps, form an extremely picturesque costume and are seen to great advantage when the men are in a body'. Hill retired from the Army in 1851 and died unmarried three years later.

Thomas Whittingham, a farmer, lived at the hall from about 1842. He came from Middlewich where he had been one of the founders of the local Sunday School. He was a member of the Manchester and Liverpool Agricultural Society and judged the sheep competitions. He won prizes for his own produce on the 300-acre estate, and died in 1877.

Whittingham was the victim of two fires started deliberately in the out-buildings. The first, in September 1850, was started by a man known as 'Bacco Jack' after a dispute with Whittingham's son. The following month, Whittingham and other farmers received threatening letters to burn their farms down if they continued to employ Irish labour. Then in June 1865 the hay barns were set alight.

On an agricultural tour of local farms in August 1856 the Manchester Courier reported: 'Ashley Hall is a fine old building, reduced one third from its size in former days. It is approached through an avenue of venerable walnut trees, and surrounded on every side, but that facing Bowdon, of which an excellent view is had, by majestic timber, very extensive kitchen and flower gardens, a very spacious vinery, where thousands of bunches of grapes were fast approaching perfection. The farm... is essentially a dairy farm... and besides rearing cattle, it supports upwards of forty milch cows ... Our explorations at an end we sat down to tea, presided over by the Misses Whittingham, and having done ample justice to hams, joints etc, so liberally provided, with regret we left...'

The high standards of farming at the hall were maintained by the next tenant Charles Sherwin, who gained the reputation of being one of the finest agriculturalists in the north of England. In 1881, he employed 9 men, 3 women and 3 boys at the farm. A visitor to the estate in 1887 described the house and garden as being in 'excellent order' with an impressive entrance hall and a carved black staircase.

Front door and one of the inner doors

He won about 3000 prizes for his cattle, as well as many awards for the best-regulated farm. He was also a cattle judge at shows and

Above: Remains of a walled garden

Below: The present outer wall used to be attached to a gable which was demolished in 1972

a member of the Royal Agricultural Society and other local societies. Locally, he was chairman of the Ashley district, warden at the Parish Church, and manager of the schools. He was also quartermaster for the Yeomanry and a Freemason. A large fire in 1888, thought to have been started by a spark from a threshing machine, destroyed stock and damaged outbuildings totalling around £2000. He died in 1900 aged 56, and the farm continued under the management of his widow Emma, until she left to run a guest house in Southport.

Henry Lowe, who next farmed at Ashley Hall, was also considered to be an authority on agriculture. He came from Runcorn where he was on the Board of Guardians and farmed at Ashley for fourteen years with the help of his family until his death in 1914 aged 75.

The right-hand gable, removed in 1972 after Mr Brooks purchased the estate, contained a ballroom, chapel and billiard room. The hall was said to have secret rooms from times of religious persecution, and a rumoured priest's escape passage. Within the existing small cellar, there is a bricked-off door. Old photographs show two stone sphinxes guarding the front door.

The stone (right) outside the former smithy on Ashley Mill Lane is known as the highwayman's mounting stone. There is a legend that Dick Turpin robbed and murdered a lawyer at New Bridge Hollow near the River Bollin and then rode off to Hoo Green in the parish of Rostherne. Here he deliberately hit an ostler in the face and asked the time in order to give the impression that he was not at the scene of the crime. Turpin once reputedly stayed at the 'Saracen's Head' inn at Warburton.

The stone could have been used by 'Highwayman Higgins' from nearby Knutsford who muffled his horse's feet with stockings to make surprise attacks on his victims. Romper Lowe of Bowdon and his gang also operated in the vicinity. His technique was to get others to commit crimes while he was being closely watched by the local constables.

Shepherd's Cottages, Bowdon (left) was the scene of a highway robbery when a farm servant on his way by horse and cart from Knutsford to Manchester, stopped for a rest. He was attacked and robbed of his money but also his bread and cheese lunch wrapped in a handkerchief. The thieves were later caught with their ill-gotten gains and convicted on the evidence of the dairymaid who made the cheese. She testified it tasted strongly of seasoning which was confirmed when it was sampled in court.

Coppice Farm tithe barn, on Ashley Mill Lane, is thought to date back to at least the 15th century. An 1839 map refers to it as 'Coppy Farm'

Clibrans, market gardeners, rented the property from the Tatton Estate until 1967 when it was taken over by Newton's nursery

Four beam hooks on which the tithes were hung are to be seen inside the barn with its massive oak box-frame construction

The cruck barn has been renovated and is now the office and showroom of Interior Plantscapes who supply plant displays for offices

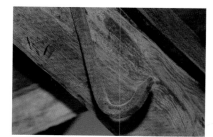

Tithe hook

Old cheese press at the side of the barn

The earlier oak weather boards

Ashley Mill

It is thought to have been a much later corn mill than Castle Mill or Bollington, and is not shown on 18th-century maps. The mill was operating in the early 1800s because John Neild, the miller in 1815, was complaining to Samuel Greg at Styal mill as Greg had stopped the flow of the river for his own purposes, thus causing problems at Ashley.

John Hope Neild inherited the mill from his father but he left in about 1836. He had financial problems but became manager of the Manchester and Salford Savings Bank, presumably installed by his Uncle, William Neild, who was the Chairman. William was a prominent Manchester alderman who was known as 'The Father of the Council' and collapsed and died at a Town Hall sub-committee meeting in 1864. He had been Mayor of the city, a magistrate and owned calico printworks in Manchester

Top: The mill house today
Below: The mill prior to 1872

Hale Civic Society

Remains of the mill c1885

Ashley children used to stand on the railway bridge, the highest point in the village, to look towards Knutsford. On clear days they watched out for the black flag to to be raised at Knutsford prison on execution days. Around nine hangings took place between 1886 and 1912 before the prison became a military detention centre, with the last civilian prisoner leaving in 1915. The prison was demolished in 1930.

and Dukinfield through marriage. He lived at High Lawn, Bowdon and was a close friend of fellow Quaker and scientist John Dalton.

Otters were a problem for James Davenport, the miller at Ashley for twenty years. They hunted the trout in these parts and so in 1848 he trapped and killed a large otter which was stuffed and put on show in a shop in Altrincham. Otters were trapped because the local landowners had a spawning house nearby to hatch thousands of trout. Otter hunting in England and Wales became illegal in 1978.

One of Davenport's mill employees was involved in a tragic and curious drowning in 1850. Joseph Pixton aged 22 had repeatedly dreamt that he was going to drown and joked with friends and family about who should have his clothing and watch if it should come true. One hot evening he left the group with whom he had been swimming near the mill to go to a point further along the river, where he could dive into deeper water. He went in head-first but did not re-surface. The alarm was raised and despite the efforts of James Davenport, who was a good swimmer, he couldn't rescue Pixton, and the body was found an hour and a half later. By coincidence the

1851 census lists a 'Joseph Pickstone', a carter age 22, living and working at the mill the following year.

The 1872 floods washed away nearby footbridges, causing damage to the mill's internal and external wheels, the mill weir, and left the Bollin between six and ten feet deeper on this stretch of the river. William Carter, the miller, wrote to the owner Lord Egerton to request the repair of the weir. The request was politely declined because of the cost. In the census three years later, Carter, who had been there since around 1870, was still listed as the miller. However in the next census he had become solely a farmer.

By 1902 the mill was in ruins with the remains of two water-wheels still to be seen, but it was a picturesque scene and a favourite subject for artists. This stretch of the river was

Top: A correspondent wrote to the Altrincham Guardian in April 1894 warning readers about the dangerous condition of the bridge near the mill. '...half of it seems inclined to go downstream. It is somewhat of a curiosity and a study in 'mechanics' as to why it (still) stands in its present shakiness'

Below: Remains of the wheel in 1899

Hale Civic Society

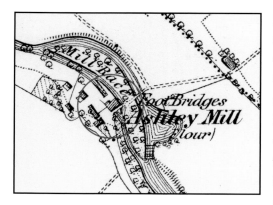

popular with many who came here on picnics and outings. A crowd of around 4000 gathered here in July 1905 to witness a baptismal service held by Hale Road Baptist Chapel. Church members sang 'Shall we gather at the river' accompanied by the church harmonium on the back of a lorry parked by the river. Pastor F Cowell Lloyd explained to the crowd what was to happen, and then went into the changing tent halfway down the river bank. Then, in his robes, he baptised the five candidates in the Bollin which was swollen and fast flowing after recent rainfall. His grandfather had the privilege of baptising the great 19th-century Baptist preacher Charles Spurgeon. This had become a familiar occasion, with many river baptisms around the country following revival in the churches.

*Ashley mill some time
after the flood of 1872*

Hale Civic Society

Millers

1815 - Correspondence between John Neild of Ashley Mill and Samuel Greg at Styal

1827 - Partnership dissolved between John Hope Neild and J Clarke

1828 - John Neild, miller

1837 - Owner: William Henry Assheton Smith, occupier: James Davenport

1857 - Son Joshua, miller

1864 - Joshua Davenport, miller, corn dealer and poor rate collector

1869 - George Wood

1871 - William Carter, miller employing ten men

1901 - Son, Thomas, Ashley Mill, farmer

Top: *The river Bollin at Ashley mill*

Middle: *Remains of the mill*

Above: *Cuckoo flower*

Left: *Remains of the mill race c1885*

The river Bollin at Ashley Mill was a favourite spot, especially on bank holidays and weekends with Sunday School parties. The site today is surrounded by trees.

Wild snowdrops

Birkin Brook on the right as it flows into the river Bollin at Bowdon near Castle Hill. The Birkin, which is popular with anglers, rises at Knutsford and is joined by Mobberley Brook, Sugar Brook and Tatton Mere Brook shortly before entering the Bollin

Birkin Brook

Watch Hill

The earthwork is from Norman times when around 750 of these castles were built across the country to consolidate the invaders' hold over the territory. They consisted of a wooden tower on the mound surrounded by a timber wall, along with a lower protected area. A garrison would have been stationed here at this vantage point over the River Bollin, with also a deep ravine on the north side. It is close to a crossing point over the river at Watlingford.

A silver penny found in a rabbit hole on the site dates back to the time of Henry II (1154-89), which confirms the castle was constructed to repel local resistance. The motte and bailey are listed as an ancient monument and are considered to be of national importance.

The Bollin from the top of the earthworks

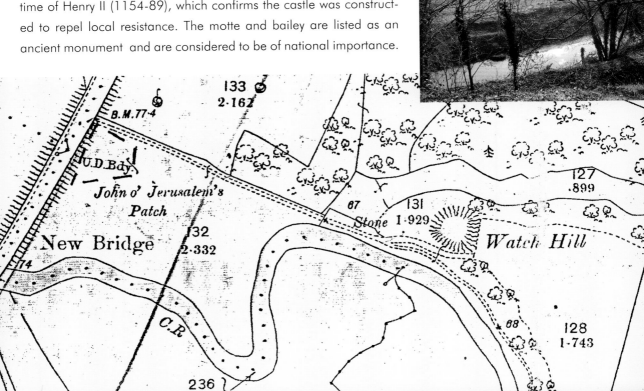

A parcel of land next to the A56 Dunham
Road close to the Bowdon roundabout,
known as 'John O' Jerusalem's Patch'.
It is now part of the Dunham Massey estate
owned by the National Trust but its name
suggests Knight's Templar associations.

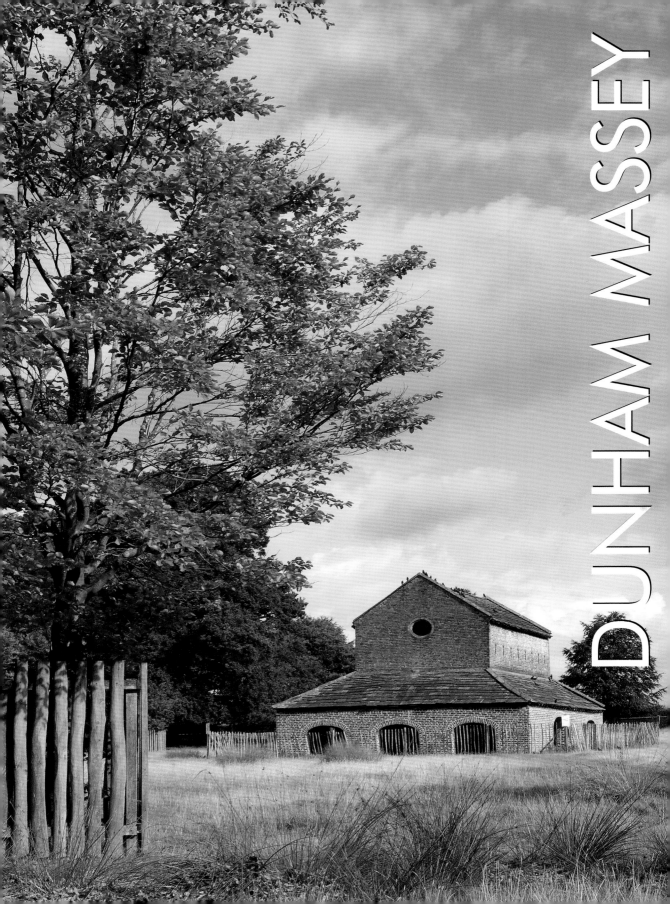

DUNHAM MASSEY

Dunham Massey

It is comprised of Dunham Massey Hall estate, along with the villages of Dunham Town, Dunham Woodhouses, Sinderland Green and the residential district of Oldfield Brow. 'Massey' is derived from the name of the Maci family who were the baronial owners in the medieval period.

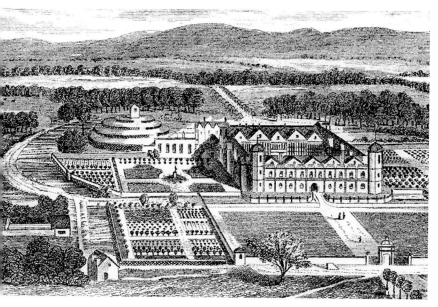

Previous page: The 1740 deer barn

Above: Dunham in 1697 showing the raised mound next to the hall

Opposite top: There is a saying that the two lions from the Booth crest, guarding the hall, raise a paw when they hear the clock on the carriage house strike twelve - the catch is of course that they don't hear.

Opposite below: The carriage clock and clock tower were built in the 1730s along with a new kitchen block and orangery.

Opposite: The previous roof line of the hall before it was lowered to include the fashionable dormer windows and give a more pleasing design to the frontage.

Domesday book referred to 'Duneham' as formerly belonging to Eluard, a Saxon freeman. The hall was the likely site of the home of the de Massey family, lords of the manor in Norman times. From this raised position there would be a commanding view over the River Bollin. The mound to the north-west of the hall may have been the situation of the first castle. It is shown in earlier drawings as being much higher than it is today. However, the Watch Hill mound near the point where the Bollin is crossed by the Roman Road between Manchester and Chester could also be the castle at Dunham referred to in a 1332 document when it was repaired.

From the 11th century, the de Mascys would have lived in a separate hall next to the castle mound. A 1410 survey of the property states it was surrounded by a moat, but there is no mention of a castle. It had probably been a two-storey building comprising a ground floor hall and a chamber above. Substantial rebuilding of the hall began in about 1580 with 'Old' Sir George Booth the first of his family to live in the new brick-built three-winged mansion. The 1648 court roll shows that he had also built barns, mills, gardens and stables. His grandson 'Young' Sir George made further improvements and it became one of the eight largest houses in the county.

George Booth, the second Earl of Warrington, had the hall rebuilt for the fourth time in the 1730s in the Georgian style. It was built on the footprint of the former building, at the same time as many thousands of trees were planted throughout the park as part of the grand design. Work began on building the wall which surrounds the park in 1748 and took three years to complete. Additional buildings were constructed such as the carriage block, orangery, deer house and kitchen block. Booth also endowed the hall with fine silver and furniture. In 1736 the hall passed by marriage into the Grey family, with Harry the 4th Earl of Stamford. Following his Grand Tour in 1760 many paintings were brought to the hall by the 5th Earl.

The 1820s saw the building of the bow-fronted windows on the east front, and staircase on the north front. The hall remained unaltered from 1855 until 1906 when the 9th Earl of Stamford returned to live there. Architect Joseph Compton Hall lowered the roof line on the south side to incorporate dormer windows, and designed the new three-tiered front portico. Inside, the hall was substantially redecorated and re-furnished.

Roger Grey, the 10th Earl, brought back to Dunham silver, furniture and paintings that had been dispersed. After his death in 1976, Dunham Massey was given to the National Trust.

William Grey, the ninth Earl of Stamford with his wife Penelope the Countess, and children Roger and Jane. He was born in Newfoundland and inherited the title from his uncle Harry who lived in South Africa. Henry, the first Earl, was a commander in the Parliamentary army during the Civil War. His eldest son Richard was one of the judges who signed the warrant for the execution of Charles I.

In 1906, following extensive restoration and modernisation, the family moved into the hall, receiving an enthusiastic welcome from the tenants and the dignitaries of Altrincham, Hale and Bowdon, and the local Court Leet. He had dedicated his life to helping others, but only lived a further five years, after contracting pernicious anaemia in 1910 on one of his humanitarian journeys.

*There were comments that the 2nd Earl was being extravagant planting
100,000 trees as part of his grand design for the park at Dunham, but
he wisely replied that they would be appreciated by later generations*

*The bridge to the garden has been removed, but the foundations
can still be seen below the surface of the lake*

Above: Visitors to Dunham Massey in 1908

Left: The old corn mill which had been operating from 1616 was converted into a saw mill about 1860. It has a working water wheel and was used to cut timber until 1905. The brick building is said be the oldest in Trafford. The mill machinery has been recently reconstructed and restored.

Right: In 1714 the 2nd Earl of Warrington placed an obelisk at the end of an avenue of trees known as Langham Grove, in memory of his mother. Another obelisk, which can be seen from the hall by the Bridgewater Canal, was said to commemorate a favourite racehorse of the Earl of Stamford which won many races wearing gold shoes.

'The Big Tree' has been a feature here at Dunham Town for over two hundred years, and villagers mounted a campaign to save it when the local authority wanted to remove it in 1977. It was claimed that the lime tree was dying but it was not clear whether it belonged to the Dunham Massey estate or the council. The tree was reprieved and continues to grow although some boughs have been lopped off and the centre of the trunk filled with concrete to prevent further deterioration.

Hale Civic Society

THIS SCHOOL was Erected in 1759 For the Benefit of the Township of *Dunham Massey* According to the Will of THOMAS WALTON Gent:

Little Heath School, Dunham Town, built by the donation of Thomas Walton, an attorney (see page 174) who left an estate of around £15,000. He gave money for the founding of two schools in Dunham Massey. Children from three to seven were taught here along with those who paid fees. A bigger school was built next to it in 1894 as numbers grew. The original school closed in 1953 and the other building became the village hall.

The Dunham Massey Brewing Company began in 2007 in a converted barn behind Big Tree farm. They produce traditionally brewed beer, with no added sugars, which is on sale at the brewery shop on Oldfield Lane, and in pubs around the area.

The spent grain is recycled for cattle food, and the hops into fertiliser at nearby Little Heath Farm.

Regular beers include: Deer Beer, Big Tree Bitter, Stamford Bitter and Little Bollington Bitter. Dunham Spice and Bowdon Parish Ale are some of the seasonal brews.

Above: The Bridgewater canal at Dunham. The Countess of Stamford rather hastily approved the Duke of Bridgewater's proposed route of his canal through the Dunham Massey estate. Later she insisted that it should not cut through their parkland nor was he to divert the River Bollin into the canal.

Below: Score marks, caused by the friction of the towing rope on horse-drawn boats, can be seen on the side of the bridge at Little Heath. Hardened blue bricks were used on the corner. Goods to and from Dunham Hall, and 'night soil' were unloaded at the wharf here.

Left & below: Manor Farm, Dunham Woodhouses, was a Dower House, built by the Earl of Warrington in the 18th century. His portrait hung in the hall for two hundred years, and many of the nineteen rooms are oak-panelled. A visitor to the house remembers one room being padded, although it is not known why. It was the home of Thomas Walton, steward to the 2nd Earl of Warrington. He was also a salt merchant and was responsible for Dunham Woodhouse's growth as a salt village. Walton died in 1757 and his name is scratched on a window.

The village farmhouse opposite Manor farm is thought to have been the home of a local official. It is said to have a beautiful oak staircase, and is a good example of a 'double depth' house introduced in the early 17th-century for the higher social classes.

Salt worker's cottage, Dunham Woodhouses

Above: The Bollin looking back towards the Dunham Aqueduct

Left: Saltworking at Dunham was established by the Booth family in the 1620s. This is the possible site of one of the 17th-century brine and salt springs on an old route of the Bollin.

Thomas Walton's will refers to salt pans, boilers and cisterns here at the workings

The maize maze at Red House farm, where there is also a farm shop, tea room, children's play area and other special events. The 155-acre farm is owned by the National Trust. The maize hedges grow to about 8ft, and are replanted to a new design each year. Entrants to the maze are given a red flag, in case of difficulty.

Fish return to the Bollin

Over the last twenty-five years the water quality of the Bollin and surrounding rivers has significantly improved following a clean up of the waterways. Just a few years previously, the Mersey had been one of the most polluted rivers in Europe and fish could not survive there. But now more fish are being seen

in the river. A 2004 newspaper article featured the story of a Prestbury resident who had seen salmon jumping the weir by Styal Mill in the river Bollin. This was thought to be the first sighting for over a century.

Above: Brown trout, below: Chub

The Environment Agency report that twelve species have been recorded in the Bollin, and a local angling club have caught 8lb trout in the river. Atlantic Salmon are returning to the Mersey and swimming up the Bollin. They have been observed at Heatley Mill where there is now a river pass, although there are eleven barriers before reaching the river Dean, which is an important spawning and rearing area for salmon. There are also fish passes at Little Bollington weir (opposite page) and another at Styal Mill weir. A study by the Environment Agency in 2010 showed that six salmon tagged at Woolston weir on the Mersey had found their way into the Bollin.

Photography: Environment Agency

LITTLE BOLLINGTON

(Left) The unusual pub name originates from the time of Elizabeth I who allowed the wine-merchants guild to take ownership of some of the royal swans. In order to distinguish between the monarch's and the vintner's swans, they were marked on their beaks. The royals had one knife nick and the vintners two - hence the pub's name.

Today the royal swans are not marked, but the guild of dyers were later given permission to own swans and used the single nick.

Over the centuries, the name has been slightly twisted and there are pubs with the name of 'the Swan with two necks'.

The inn at Bollington was known as 'The Swan' until about 1929 when it changed to its present name.

(Below) 15th-century White Cottage is thought to be the oldest house in Bollington and once the home of the local bailiff. It was renovated by the National Trust in 1994 and part of it is now a tea-room.

Face carved on to the side of the bridge of the Bridgewater Canal at Little Bollington

Little Bollington Mill

The mill is the only surviving corn mill structure on the river. It was first mentioned in 1260 in the Chester County Court Rolls, and by 1380 was one of the mills owned by the barony of Dunham Massey with also a fishery at the site. 15th-century documents showed that Henry de Mascy, bailiff of the manor, held the mill at a cost of £4 6s 8d and the fishing rights for trapping eels at 2s. The income for selling 504 eels in around 1412 came to 5s 8d. In 1413 the mill had been re-built in timber at a cost of £4 16s.

The mill can be seen in an 18th-century painting of Dunham Park but it is a different structure from the present building. In 1776, 'Bollington Mills' (there was both a corn and a meal mill here) were advertised to be let. They contained 'one pair of French stones and three pairs of grey stones (for grinding), a pair of malt rollers, drying kiln, a dressing mill, and every proper convenience for the grinding of corn, malt and grain; drying of oats, and dressing flour and meal'. The advertisement also mentioned the availability of a 'convenient

Mill race

dwelling house' near the mill. A 1790 lease between the Earl of Stamford and farmer Samuel Walker of Dunham Woodhouses for the 'Bollington Mills' on the 'River Bollen', granted the rights to any fish found in the dams and sluices.

The mill had burnt down in the 1780s, and in January 1847 the later building suffered the same fate. The miller, Peter Walker, had been working late at the mill until 11pm on the Friday night but at 5.30am the next morning, when other staff arrived, they found part of the mill in flames. The fire engine from Dunham Hall was brought but within two hours of discovering the fire, despite the efforts of the villagers, nothing was left of the mill except the walls. 500 sacks of ground and unground flour, valued at around £1000, were lost. A kiln adjoining the building was saved, along with some corn. It was noted that this was the third incident in recent weeks, with fires at Arley and Dee (Chester) corn mills. Although there were suspicions about a mysterious man looking through a window in a nearby house the night before, it was thought that the fire had been caused by friction from the machinery, and the fire insurance company paid up.

In December 1855 John Davenport, a corn dealer living at 26-28 Church Street East, Altrincham, acquired a 999-year leasehold tenure agreement for the site. He had been born at Northenden corn mill in 1813, where his father was the miller. His father went on to manage Castle Mill and then Ashley Mill.

The mill from the Bridgewater Canal

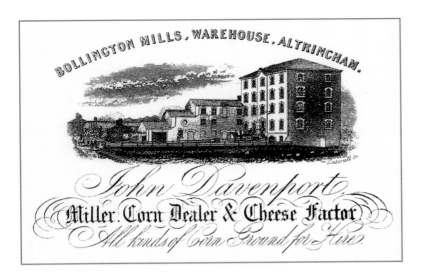

Davenport rebuilt the mill at Bollington and his business was first listed there in the 1857 postal directory. By 1861 he had six millers and two apprentice boys in his employment. Robert Peel, an employee of Davenport, suffered severe injuries in an accident at the mill in October 1868 when he lost most of his toes in machinery. He had been standing on a cog wheel when he slipped but managed to hang onto an iron bar to prevent even worse injury. Peel was taken, on what must have been an extremely painful journey by train, to be treated at the Manchester Royal Infirmary.

Bridgewater Canal

John Davenport was prominent in public life - he was a Liberal in politics and elected Mayor of Altrincham in 1855. He was one of the founders, directors and latterly chairman of the Altrincham Gas Company. He regularly exhibited at the Altrincham Rose Show and became the first chairman of the local Agricultural Society. He was a member of the Court Leet, served on the Local Board and was a trustee of the Mayor's Land Charity.

The side of the mill by the Bollin

It was said that he had an unrivalled knowledge of local events from the past and delighted in sharing his memories with anyone who would listen. In addition to his other roles, he was on the Hospital and Dispensary committee, attended Dunham Road Unitarian Chapel and was a Freemason at the Knutsford Lodge. After retiring from business in 1887, he went to live at 3 Burlington Place Altrincham. On the day of his funeral in November 1902, the shops were closed out of respect for this popular well-known local figure who died at the age of ninety.

In the Rev Agate's funeral address for John Davenport he said '...in various capacities and in quiet and unostentatious fashion, he served the community among whom he dwelt. A man of simple speech and habits, straightforward and direct in his dealings, and with a kindly heart, he journeyed the round of life, doing almost to the last, such work as long experience had qualified him to perform, and never losing his interest in the things that had occupied his years of vigour'. His son John lived at the Mill House, Bollington with his family in 1881 but left three years later to become the manager of Longlands corn mill at Slaithwaite.

Bollington Mill was purchased by George Richards and Company, Broadheath. They had to suspend production in April 1894 after the walls of the mill race collapsed during work to repair the weir. Workmen had to run to safety as the workings fell apart. The following Sunday, hundreds came to view the scene of devastation - parts of an adjoining garden of fruit trees, and sections of the river bank which had also fallen into the Bollin, and a damaged bridge.

The following year the mill was auctioned. It had a capacity for up to six sacks an hour, and was equipped with six pairs of grinding stones, boiler, engine and water wheel. There was a good farmers' trade of offals and grist. George Evans managed the mill for forty years until his death in June 1936 at the age of 80. He was a member of Manchester Corn Exchange, and had a specialist interest in breeding

Bollington Mill 1988

Hazel Pryor

The river Bollin looking towards Little Bollington Mill

Jersey and Friesian cattle. For many years he had been chairman of the parish council. The mill had been for sale in 1933, but after Evans' death it was put up for auction as a going concern the following September.

The mill was modernised in 1938 and continued production until after the last War when it became a provender mill, also selling cattle food. S Kenworthy Ltd, corn merchants who had a warehouse at Victoria Avenue Timperley, are listed at Bollington from about 1966, using it for storage and the distribution of agricultural and horticultural supplies. By this time the mill machinery and the wheels had been removed.

The mill was put up for sale in 1980 and was to remain derelict until a planning application for change of use was submitted in March 1987 to turn the listed building into flats. Permission was granted, and the building, which by then was in a poor condition, was converted by Kingsley Homes into eight apartments and four mews houses, with swimming pool, saunas, gymnasium and solariums. Various outbuildings on the property, considered to detract from the main mill, were demolished.

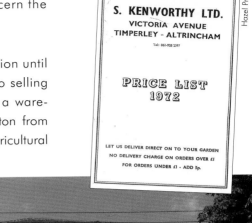

The empty mill 1987

Millers

1776 - Mill to let	and corn dealer employing 4 millers and 2 apprentice boys	1923 - George Evans & Son
1828-34 - George Walker		1936 - Mill sold by auction
1837 - Tithe map - owned by Earl of Stamford, occupied by Martha Walker	1881 - Son John living at mill house with wife and family	1938 - Modernised
	1884 - Mill Cottage to let	1939 - A Oakes
1841 - John Morten	1887 - Auction for horses, lurries and effects from the mill	1942 - Herbert Allen
1847 - Mill fire, miller - Peter Walker of Bollington	1892 - Richards & Co, millers	1973 - S Kenworthy, horticultural sundries (he had been listed from 1966 as corn merchant with warehouse Victoria Avenue, Timperley)
1857 - PO Directory, J Davenport	1894 - Mill owned by George Richards & Co Broadheath	
1861 - John Davenport, 28 Church St Altrincham - miller	1898 - George Evans	1987 - Change of use.

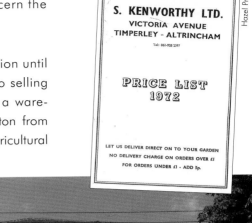

S. KENWORTHY LTD.
VICTORIA AVENUE
TIMPERLEY - ALTRINCHAM
Tel: 061-928 2397

PRICE LIST
1972

LET US DELIVER DIRECT ON TO YOUR GARDEN
NO DELIVERY CHARGE ON ORDERS OVER £1
FOR ORDERS UNDER £1 - ADD 5p.

Hazel Pryor

Hazel Pryor

Dunham Aqueduct

The aqueduct which takes the Bridgewater Canal over the River Bollin was completed by 1769. The canal narrows as it goes over the Bollin, 34 feet below, to reduce the weight of water on the structure.

The stability of the structure has been an ongoing problem. In 1814, the Earl of Stamford was advised by his steward that it was in grave danger of collapse and was being strengthened. A huge leak in the canal was reported by two boys early one morning in 1971. In spite of prompt action to close the leak with stop logs, millions of gallons of water poured out of the canal creating a 90 ft gorge in the embankment and flooding the surrounding fields. The water loss caused the canal level in Manchester to drop 14 inches.

A Trust comprised of county and local authorities was set up to share the costs of repairs and maintenance. It took two years and £250,000 to repair the damage.

WARBURTON

Wheat and barley growing on land close to the Trans-Pennine route. The wheat is taken to Manchester where it is used in artificial sweetener products. The field is on a former flood plain and is occasionally under water in winter. The farmer remembers standing on the bridge (see below) watching a cormorant catching fish in the river Bollin.

Trans-Pennine Trail

The trail which runs through the Bollin valley is part of a long distance route stretching 350 miles between Hornsea on the Yorkshire coast near Hull, to Southport on the Lancashire coast.

The Trafford section opened in 1998 for the use of walkers, cyclists and horse-riders, following the purchase of land. The trail links with other long-distance paths starting in Ireland and connecting with routes which reach Switzerland, Turkey and Russia. The idea for the trail originated in Barnsley to make use of disused railway lines.

The Bollin as it passes beneath the trail at Warburton

The Trans-Pennine Trail runs along the route of the old Warrington-Stockport railway which opened in 1835. The station buildings at Heatley still remain

The coming of the railway to Lymm contributed to its growth, as Manchester merchants chose to live there, away from the grime of the city

The line closed for passenger traffic under the 'Beeching axe' in 1962, by which time its main use was taking supporters to watch cricket and football at Old Trafford

Goods trains continued to run along the line taking coal to Fiddlers Ferry power station and Garston Docks, Liverpool

Heatley Mill

The mill was one of the earliest medieval mills in northern Cheshire with references to it in a charter of 1170. It probably stood about 40m to the north-east of the last mill possibly on an earlier course of the river - marked on maps as the 'Old Bollin'. The sandstone foundations of an earlier mill could be seen by Bollin bridge when water levels were low. The Warburton to Lymm road once forded the river at this point. The mill was rebuilt in 1716, according to diarist Arnold Drinkwater. When it was advertised to be let in December 1833, it was described as 'valuable and desirable'.

It had been part of the Warburton estates for many centuries, with the River Bollin supplying a continuous and plentiful supply of water power. There were three other water-powered mills on the vast Warburton estates. The Egerton Warburton family lived at Arley Hall and sold the mill to the CWS in 1918.

Below: Drawing of the mill before alterations to the roof and further extensions. The mill was lit by oil lamps and candles until 1905. The burn marks could be seen on the beams in later years.

Bottom: The apartments built on the site of the mill

Thornley family

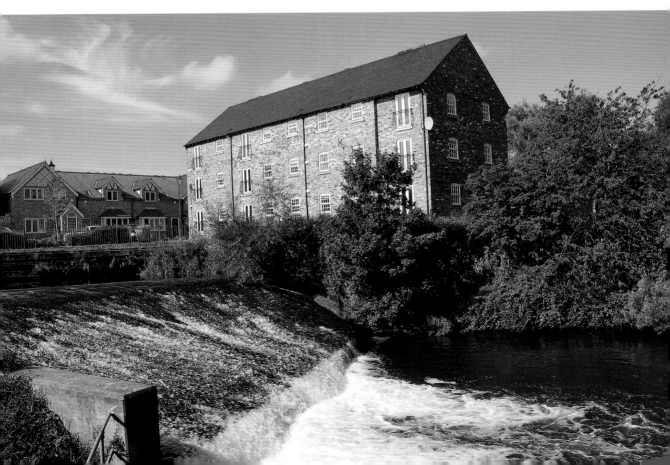

Thornley family

Warburton mill yard 1937

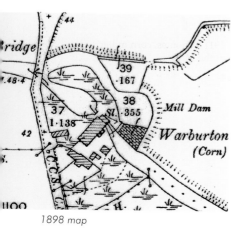

1898 map

The last four-storey mill building had been constructed sometime between 1825 and 1870. The sandstone foundations suggest it was rebuilt on the site of an earlier mill. The mill had a water wheel for use during normal water levels and another for high water.

Alongside the 19th-century mill, there was a mill house and a range of buildings from the 1930s to 1950, when a long warehouse to store animal feeding-stuffs and fertilisers was built. The two water wheels were replaced by a Swiss water turbine engine in 1905 which remained in operation until the closure of the business.

The Thornleys were the last family to own and operate the mill. James Thornley from Norbury Mill, Stockport with his sons, Thomas and William, came in 1895 as tenants. He bought the building and nine acres of land from the CWS in 1931. By 1986, the mill produced about five tons of corn daily and employed ten people. The corn came from nearby farms, and they supplied oats, barley, wheat, as well as fertilizer and pet food.

190

To Corn Dealers,
MILLERS, AND OTHERS.
TO BE LET BY TICKET,
AT THE
Crown Inn, in Northwich,
IN THE COUNTY OF CHESTER.
On SATURDAY, the 28th of December, 1833,
At the Hour of Four in the Afternoon; subject to certain Conditions, and for a Term of Years, if required;
ALL THAT VALUABLE AND DESIRABLE
Water Corn Mill,
CALLED
WARBURTON MILL,

Situate in WARBURTON, in the said County of Chester, with the House, Outbuildings, and Appurtenances thereunto belonging; as the same are now occupied by Messrs. LEIGH and HARDY.

The above Mill is situate on the River Bollin, close to the Duke of Bridgewater's Canal, and the Mersey and Irwell Navigation, and within the distance of twelve miles from Manchester, on excellent Roads. It is worked by two Undershut Wheels, and contains five pair of Stones, with all usual and necessary Utensils, Machinery, and Tackling.

To view the same apply at the Mill, or to Mr. GRACE, Arley Hall, near Northwich; and for further particulars, at the Office of Mr. HOSTAGE, Solicitor, Castle-Northwich.

PRINTED AT THE OFFICE OF F. CARNES, NORTHWICH.

Thornley family

Thornley family

Millers

1828 - Severe flooding in July

1828-9 - Pigot, John Leigh, miller in previous business partnerships - Richard Gibson and Samuel Gibson dissolved 12 May 1807, and with Richard Gibson until 3 February 1815.

1837 - Tithe map, owner: Rowland Eyles Egerton Warburton, occupier: John Leigh

1850 - Directory, Walker and Fletcher

1851 - Samuel Walker and cousin George Fletcher

1857 - William Shaw, miller and corn dealer

1864 - Directory, William Shaw, miller and corn dealer

1874 - Directory Robert Linton, miller and corn dealer

1879 - Newspaper report of man found drowned near Mill

1881 - Robert Linton, miller and corn dealer at Mill Cottage

1891 - William Horsefield, corn miller at Mill House

1892 - Joshua Slater

1896 - Thornley family from Norbury Mill, Stockport

1901 - James Thornley, corn miller at the Mill House

1911 - Thomas, corn miller at the Mills

1929 - Severe flooding prevented the water-wheel working

1930 - J Thornley and Sons

Above top: Flooding c1948 by the building where hay was crushed and chopped

Left: Company lorry 1930

Above: Silo construction 1935 which had eight bins, each holding twenty tons of grain

Below: Mill yard and workers, with the traction engine driving machinery filling the sacks

The business continued in the ownership of the Thornleys, but following the changes in agriculture and the rising costs of the upkeep of the mill, they re-located to Burley Heyes Mill Appleton in 1991 to become retailers.

The property was sold in 1991 to North West Water who planned to transform the mill into offices and the four and a half-acre site into their new headquarters. However, this was not realized and the land was bought by a housing developer. The disused mill had become unsafe and was dismantled between September and December 1999. By April 2000, Roland Bardsley Homes had rebuilt the former mill as the 'Old Mill' apartments in the same style on the site. The mill had been regarded as one of the best surviving examples of its type in the region.

Top: Mill c1960

Above: Fish pass at Heatley mill

Below: Mill interior c1960. At this time, grain-drying plant had to be installed with the introduction of combine harvesters

Above: The mill cottage (right) was originally two dwellings. It was made into one when the Thornleys arrived. In 1910 Thomas remained there while other family members moved into homes around the village.

Thomas and Ada Thornley 1928

Above: Roger, Frank, John and Thomas Thornley 1976

Right: Company outing to the London Festival of Britain 1953. Back row - Thomas Thornley (left), Frank Thornley (glasses), John Thornley (right)

Above and inset: Heatley bridge, one of the best along the Bollin with a fine gothic arch. The other side is much plainer following bridge repairs.

The bridge had been rebuilt in about 1862 after its foundations had been damaged by frequent flooding

The river here is 45ft above sea level compared to 1280ft where it originated

Right: The 'Little Bollin' opposite Heatley Mill which was the original route of the river. (It can be seen at the top of the map on page 190)

(Left) The 16th-century Saracen's head inn where highwayman Dick Turpin reputedly slept in a four-poster bed in a secret room. There was said to be a wife-market nearby where spouses were exchanged or sold.

(Below) Architect John Douglas whose work is seen throughout Cheshire and North Wales

Wall slabs held together with metal cramps

Parish room designed by John Douglas

Warburton

At the centre of the village are the old steps which was once a meeting place for the local traders. Nearby are the traditional slabstone walls of sandstone. One of them is reputed to contain the footprints of a dinosaur. The village is sometimes nicknamed 'Douglas Land' because the Victorian architect, John Douglas, was responsible for quite a number of buildings here, including the 'new' church, Bent farm, the school and village houses. He is regarded as Cheshire's finest architect and designed in the Arts and Crafts style. The medieval appearance of Chester is largely attributed to him and he also designed the iconic Eastgate clock. An Elizabethan wall painting was discovered at nearby Onion Farm, which depicted the legendary 8th century St Werburgh and a goose. She reputedly restored a goose to life, and her shrine at Chester Cathedral was popular with pilgrims.

The base of the stone cross and the stocks which may be from the 17th century

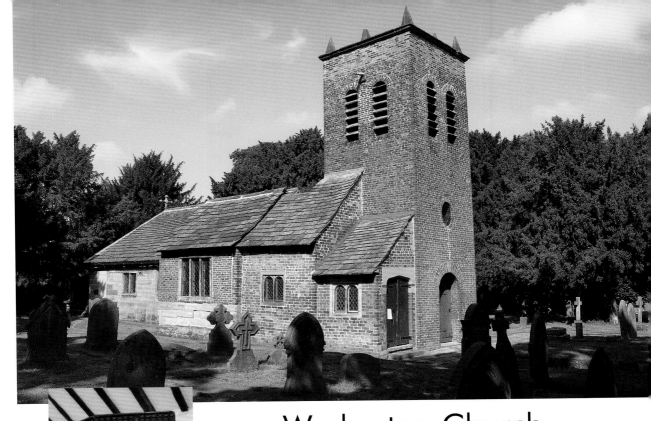

Warburton Church

St Werburgh's church is the oldest surviving building in Warburton and one of the earliest timber-framed churches in the county. It was possibly built on the site of a Saxon church. There was also a priory here between 1179 and 1790 and the three stone coffins found in 1816 are from the 12th century. The church is a mixture of architectural periods, the oldest being the timber-framed north wall which is thought to be 12th century.

Some of the walls were rebuilt in stone in 1645 followed by the brick tower and vestry in 1711. Until the 18th century, the roof would been thatched before stone flags were used. By 1722 the floor was flagged and there would have been an annual rushbearing service when the rushes were renewed (see Macclesfield Forest Chapel). The interior wooden beams go back to the 16th century, although timbers affected by death watch beetle were replaced in 1927 and 1958.

The church was in such poor condition by 1880, that a new church was built costing £9000. In 1971, with the old church not needed for worship, it was taken over by the Churches Conservation Trust which protects historic churches at risk.

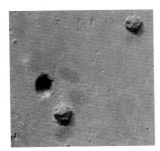

Hexagonal 16th century pulpit

Spy hole in the door to watch out for body snatchers

19th century sanctuary tiles

Door which once led to stairs up to a gallery

In the graveyard, a head-stone reads 'Under this stone lieth the bones of a virtuous woman'. Another, probably for a pet, simply reads 'Snap 1888 -1898'. One headstone records twins who died in 1814 age 72 within two months of each other.

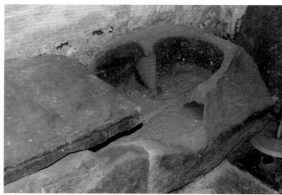

Stone coffin discovered in 1816

The Drinkwaters were local bailiffs here for two centuries

Warburton toll bridge

Although the bridge crosses the Manchester Ship Canal, the toll is paid for going over the route of the river Mersey, which once flowed through the village. It is the only toll road in Greater Manchester and one of a small number of toll bridges in the country.

Two painters came to work on the bridge in a drunken state in 1897. When they were stopped from working, one stripped off and attempted to dive 75ft into the canal. While he was being restrained with ropes, the other worker suddenly jumped into the water and drowned. The surviving painter was fined 20s.

The first bridge over the Mersey built in 1863 was in place of the Hollins Ferry. This was filled in to become a ramp for the new bridge of the Ship Canal in 1884.

The old toll-house

The toll bridge, operated by the Ship Canal owners as a private statutory undertaking, has long been a source of frustration for motorists who have to travel across it in peak traffic periods when there can be long delays. The alternative route is a ten-mile detour.

Above: Remains of the landing stage where the Manchester night soil was unloaded to spread on the fields

There have been a number of attempts to end the toll. Various local authorities supported the abolition in 1905, and the following year the Motor Union succeeded in reducing the toll from 2 to 1 shilling per car. In 1934 the Ministry of Transport unsuccessfully proposed to free all of the country's 37 toll bridges. When the toll rose by 2p to 12p in 2007, there were calls for the toll to be scrapped.

Lymm

A popular centre for visitors with its picturesque village centre and canal-side walks. Lymm Dam, formed after the construction of the Stockport to Warrington turnpike road in 1824, is another attraction. The archway on Crouchley Lane near the lake is the former entrance to the Beechwood estate owned by Manchester cotton merchant George Dewhurst. Soap manufacturer William Lever later bought the estate, with plans to begin local salt production. He planted

The village hosts a number of annual events including the Easter duck race, rush-bearing, summer festival, September produce show, Dickensian Christmas and Carols at the Cross.

avenues of Lombardy Poplar trees and built an impressive bridge in the gorge in anticipation of the influx of workers. However no works or homes were built, after a suspected deal with business rivals ICI. Just below the dam there are the remains of a slitting mill where iron was cut up to be made into nails, and later into bands around beer and gunpowder barrels.

Arch to the Dewhust estate

Above: The Bollin near Reddish Hall, looking back towards St Werburgh's Church Warburton. The giant hogweed seen here on the right of the photograph is an invasive species which, along with Japanese knotweed and Himalayan balsam, is damaging the natural ecosystem along the banks of the river. They were introduced by Victorian botanists as specimen garden plants but have spread into the countryside. The giant hogweed is highly toxic and can cause blistering if touched. It is making some river-side paths virtually impassable. The Bollin Environmental group - BEACON is heading efforts to tackle the problem with chemical treatments and physical intervention. They welcome help from volunteers to pull up balsam in the summer months.

Right: The final stretch of the river's thirty-mile journey before the confluence with the Manchester Ship Canal.

Bollin Point

The river Bollin joins the Manchester Ship Canal at Bollin Point, southwest of Warburton. Work began on this section of the canal in 1888 with the river being diverted on a straighter course to the Ship Canal. Bends in the former Mersey and Irwell Navigation were eliminated in the new canal route. The earlier waterway allowed boats to sail from Manchester to Liverpool. Opposite Bollin Point is the Butchersfield Canal, a two-mile loop which provided a short cut on the river Mersey for the Navigation.

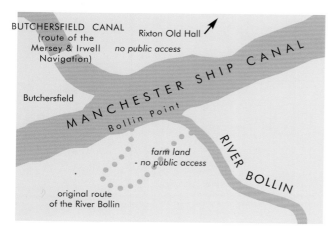

BUTCHERSFIELD CANAL
(route of the Mersey & Irwell Navigation)

Rixton Old Hall
no public access

MANCHESTER SHIP CANAL

Butchersfield

Bollin Point

RIVER BOLLIN

farm land - no public access

original route of the River Bollin

Heavy rains in November 1893 brought huge flows of water from the Bollin, causing damage and flooding further along the canal at Warrington as the water level rose by over 30ft. The Ship Canal opened the following year.

Rixton Old Hall lies on the opposite bank. It was built in 1822 and is next to the moated site of an earlier manor house. The Hall and surrounding land is occupied by a waste service company and not open to the public.

(Above left) Butchersfield Canal

(Above right) Rixton Old Hall

(Left) The earlier route of the Bollin into the Mersey with Warburton church in the distance

(Opposite page) The Bollin flowing into the Ship Canal

(Overleaf) A Mersey Ferries Ship Canal cruise at Bollin Point, going to Liverpool

Acknowledgments

With thanks for the invaluable help given by the following people, organisations and institutions:

Mike Akerman, Rev Patrick Angier - St Peter's Prestbury, Edward Blockley, Carole Bonser, Randle Brooks, Ken Broughton - The Charles Tunnicliffe Society, Rev Canon Michael Burgess - Oughtrington and Warburton parishes, Katherine Causer - Environment Agency, Cheshire Wildlife Trust, John Costello - Dunham Massey Brewery, Robert Daniels, Robert Davies, Andy Eaves - Environment Agency, Chris Frankland, Alan Hayward - Macclesfield Museums, Chris Hill, John Huddleston - The Charles Tunnicliffe Estate, Geoffrey Hunt, John Jocys, Fr Kenrick - St Peter's Stockport, Harmen Koop - United Utilities, Denise Laver - Hale Civic Society, John Lee, Brian Lyons - United Utilities, Eileen MacAulay - Pownall School, David and Alice Maddley, Mr and Mrs Mason, Derrick Murdie, Sue Nichols, Graham Pike, Angela Pownall, William Pownall, Richard Rowlands - Interior Plantscapes, Hazel Pryor, Rev Stephen Rathbone - Macclesfield Forest Chapel, Dr Mary Roberts, Pam Savage - Wilmslow Historical Society, Jeff and Pam Skinner, Rev Dr Paul Smith - St Bartholomew's Wilmslow, Sutton Hall management, John Sykes, Brian Starkey, Amanda Storey, Ron Thorn - Macclesfield Museum, Alkestis Tsilika - National Trust, Geoffrey Warburton, Arthur Williams - Biffa Waste Services Ltd, Annabel Wills - Macclesfield Museums, Lionel Willshaw, Dr Emma Wood - Environment Agency, Jean Wright, Peter Wright

Nicola Ginn, Tim Harding, Emma Haughton, Euan Murray - Bollin Valley Partnership

Birgitta Hoffmann, Kathleen Morris, Shelia Campbell, Janet Horne, John Tomlinson, Fred Dearden, Yvonne Warren, Martin Burgess, Barbara Elms, John Thompson - Wilmslow Community Archaeology

Grateful thanks to Morris Garratt, Cynthia Hollingworth, David Miller and Judith Warrender for their proof checking

Libraries & Archives: Cheshire, Chester, Greater Manchester County Record Office, Knutsford, Lancashire County Cricket Club, Macclesfield, Macclesfield Silk Museum, Manchester, Manchester University, Quarry Bank Mill, Stockport, Trafford, Warrington, Wilmslow

Publications:

A History of Hale by Robert Norman Dore, Sherratts for Hale Civic Society 1972
A History of Warburton Corn Mills by Thomas Thornley, 1990
A Lady of Cotton by David Sekers, History Press & National Trust 2013
Bollin Valley by Joan French, Willow Publishing 1984
Bollin Valley Teachers' Pack, Cheshire County Council
Bolynton - A Historical & Archaeological Survey of Little Bollington ed by Pat Faulkner
Cheshire Life
Collar House by Sylvia Stoner 1984
Discovering Wartime Cheshire 1939-1945, Cheshire County Council 1985
Dissent in Altrincham by Stephen Birchall, Author House UK Ltd 2010

Dunham Massey, The National Trust

Dunham Massey, Cheshire: a History ed. by Don Bayliss and David Miller, Country Books 2010

Glimpses of Macclesfield by Isaac Finney, 1883

Hale and Ashley the Past 100 Years, Hale Civic Society 1987

Hale Golf Club a celebration of the first century by Neal Hyde, Hale Golf Club 2003

Historical Guide to Prestbury by Joel Johnson

History of St Bartholomew's Church in the Parish of Wilmslow, 2000

Images of England: Warburton Partington and Partington by Karen Cliff and Vicki Masterson, Tempus Publishing Ltd 2002

John Thompstone of Gawsworth Mill - A History of the Thompstone Family, by Ann Laver 1987

Knutsford Prison - The Inside Story by David Woodley, Leonie Press 2002

Langley Now and Then by Thelma Whiston, Langley Methodist Church 2008

Looking Back at Wythenshawe by Jean Greatorex and Shelia Clarke, Willow Publishing 1984

Macclesfield County Express series on the Bollin Valley by 'The Stroller' the nom-de-plume of journalist Clifford Rathbone 1968

Mill Life at Styal by Nigel Dixon & Josselin Hill, Willow Publishing 1986

My Country Book by CF Tunnicliffe, The Studio 1942

Place Names of Cheshire by J McN Dodgson, Cambridge University Press 1967

Portrait of a Country Artist CF Tunnicliffe 1901-1997 by Ian Niall, Gollancz 1980

Pownall Hall and its Chapel of St Olaf by Patricia Hodson, Wilmslow Historical Society 1993

Prestbury and Its Ancient Church by John Earles, 1928

St Werburgh's Old Church by Dr Michael Nevell, The Churches Conservation Trust 2002

The Archaeology of Trafford by Michael Nevell, Trafford Council 1997

The Church of St Stephen Macclesfield, Cheshire County Council 1989

The History of Prestbury by AJS Cartmell 1977

The Social and Economic History of Styal 1750-1850 by Walter Lazenby, 1949

The Sutton St James Story by Alan Dinnis 1990

The Buildings of England - Cheshire by Clare Hartwell, Matthew Hyde, Edward Hubbard, Nikolaus Pevsner, Yale University Press 2011

The Gregs of Styal by Mary B Rose, National Trust 1978

The Quarries of the Macclesfield Area by DA Kitching, Cheshire Countryside Management Service 1977

The Social and Economic Life of Styal 1750-1850 by Walter Lazenby 1949

The Story of Collar House in the Village of Prestbury 1780-2012 by Dr Mary Roberts, 2013

The Work of John Douglas by Edward Hubbard, The Victorian Society 1991

Tunnicliffe, Oriel Ynys Môn 2011

Warburton the History of a Village by Harold Faulkner 1989

Warburton Mill, Heatley, Cheshire, an Archaeological Report of the Mill Complex, Dr Mike Nevell, Dr Peter Arrowsmith, Steve Stockley and Derek Pierce, University of Manchester Archeological Unit 1998

Wilmslow of Yesterday by Wilmslow Historical Society 1970

Websites: Arley Hall Archives, Bollin Valley Partnership, British Newspaper Archive, Charles Tunnicliffe Society, Environment Agency, Guardian Newspaper Archive, Swan With Two Nicks, Thomas Hobson family

Carving at Pownall Hall School

Stile at Newton Hall farm, Mottram St Andrew

The river Dean (left) joining the Bollin at Wilmslow